pathfinder® guide

Norfolk

W A L K S

Compiled by
John Brooks

JARROLD
publishing

Acknowledgements

I should like to thank Peter Dugdale of Norfolk County
Council for his help in checking the definitive maps and
Keith Zealand of the National Trust for his advice on Felbrigg.

Text:	John Brooks
Photography:	John Brooks
Editorial:	Ark Creative, Norwich
Design:	Ark Creative, Norwich

Series Consultant: Brian Conduit

© Jarrold Publishing 2004

x DIFFERENT FROM 2010

o|s **Ordnance Survey®** This product includes mapping data licensed
from Ordnance Survey® with the permission
of the Controller of Her Majesty's Stationery Office. © Crown
Copyright 2004. All rights reserved. Licence number 100017593.
Ordnance Survey, the OS symbol and Pathfinder are registered
trademarks and Explorer, Landranger and Outdoor Leisure are
trademarks of the Ordnance Survey, the national mapping
agency of Great Britain.

Jarrold Publishing   ISBN 0-7117-1596-3

While every care has been taken to ensure the accuracy of
the route directions, the publishers cannot accept
responsibility for errors or omissions, or for changes in
details given. The countryside is not static: hedges and
fences can be removed, field boundaries can alter, footpaths
can be rerouted and changes in ownership can result in the
closure or diversion of some concessionary paths. Also, paths
that are easy and pleasant for walking in fine conditions may
become slippery, muddy and difficult in wet weather, while
stepping stones across rivers and streams may become
impassable.

If you find an inaccuracy in either the text or maps,
please write or e-mail to Jarrold Publishing at the
addresses below.

First published 2001
by Jarrold Publishing
Revised and reprinted 2004.

Printed in Belgium
by Proost NV, Turnhout. 7/04

Jarrold Publishing
Pathfinder Guides, Whitefriars, Norwich NR3 1TR
E-mail: info@totalwalking.co.uk
www.totalwalking.co.uk

Front cover: Shotesham church
Previous page: The River Nar

Contents

The National Trust; The Ramblers'
Association; Walkers and the Law;
Countryside Access Charter; Walking
Safety; Useful Organisations;
Ordnance Survey Maps

■ Short, easy walks

■ Walks of modest
length, likely to
involve some
modest uphill
walking

■ More challenging
walks which may
be longer and/or
over more rugged
terrain, often with
some stiff climbs

Keymap

SCALE 1:384 615 or 1 INCH to about 6 MILES *1CM to 3.8KM*
KEYMAP HEIGHTS SHOWN IN FEET

Walk	Page	Start	Nat. Grid Reference	Distance	Time
Acle and Upton	18	Acle	TG 400107	4½ miles (7.2km)	2 hrs
Aylsham, A Round of	65	Aylsham	TG 191267	8½ miles (13.7km)	4 hrs
Boudicca's Way – Shotesham and Saxlingham Nethergate	50	Shotesham	TM 256990	7 miles (11.3km)	3½ hrs
Breydon Water and the Berney Arms	84	Great Yarmouth railway station	TG 519080	10 miles (16.1km)	4 hrs
Castle Rising and Roydon Common	81	Castle Rising	TF 666248	10 miles (16.1km)	4½ hrs
Denver Sluice – a three rivers walk	59	Fordham	TL 614994	7½ miles (12.1km)	3½ hrs
Great Fransham and Little Dunham	38	Great Fransham	TF 898130	6 miles (9.7km)	2½ hrs
Great Ouse from Downham Market	46	Downham Market	TF 609033	6½ miles (10.5km)	3 hrs
Hales Green from Loddon	27	Loddon	TM 362986	5 miles (8km)	2 hrs
Hardley Cross from Chedgrave	48	Chedgrave	TM 363994	6½ miles (10.5km)	3½ hrs
Horsey	24	Horsey mill	TG 456222	5 miles (8km)	2 hrs
How Hill and Ludham	40	How Hill	TG 372189	5½ miles (8.9km)	2½ hrs
Langmere and the Devil's Punchbowl	53	East Wretham	TL 912885	6 miles (9.7km)	3½ hrs
Little Ouse from Thetford	62	Thetford	TL 868830	7½ miles (12.1km)	2½ hrs
Mannington Hall, Wolterton and the Bure valley	43	Mannington Hall	TG 142329	6½ miles (10.5km)	2½ hrs
Marham Fen and the Nar Valley Way	35	Narborough	TF 749127	5½ miles (8.9km)	2½ hrs
Metton and Felbrigg Park	32	Felbrigg Park	TG 194393	5½ miles (8.9km)	2½ hrs
Northrepps from Overstrand	20	Overstrand	TG 247410	4 miles (6.4km)	2 hrs
Oxborough and Gooderstone	30	Oxborough	TF 744014	5 miles (8km)	2 hrs
Peddars Way, Fring and Sedgeford	56	Fring church	TF 735348	7 miles (11.3km)	2½ hrs
Pulhams, The two	22	Pulham Market	TM 196862	4½ miles (7.2km)	2 hrs
Reepham, Marriott's Way and Salle	69	Reepham church	TG 101228	9½ miles (15.3km)	4 hrs
Ringland and the Wensum valley	16	Ringland	TG 133140	3 miles (4.8km)	1¼ hrs
Ringstead Downs from Holme next the Sea	87	Holme next the Sea	TF 698438	10½ miles (16.9km)	5 hrs
Warham and Wighton from Wells-Next-The-Sea	78	Wells harbour	TF 940399	8½ miles (13.7km)	4 hrs
Weeting Castle from Santon Downham	75	Santon Downham	TL 815877	9½ miles (15.3km)	4 hrs
Westwick Woods and the Weavers Way	72	North Walsham railway station	TG 281298	8 miles (12.9km)	3 hrs
Wood Green from Long Stratton	14	Long Stratton	TM 196926	3 miles (4.8km)	1½ hrs

After a stretch across fields this becomes a riverside walk. Boats abound in summer, while the waterways are deserted in winter except by wildlife and fishermen. Acle has a popular market on Thursdays.

This walk follows a stream through watermeadows for much of the way so avoid walking the route after wet weather. Aylsham is a still typical Norfolk market town with a lovely church and variety of shops.

Shotesham is one of the most attractive of Norfolk villages. The route follows tracks, field paths and country roads, passing the romantic ruins of two abandoned churches en route.

This is a linear walk along the shore of a large tidal lake abounding in birdlife. However, it can easily be extended to Reedham, from where there is a regular train service to Norwich or Great Yarmouth.

This walk captures the diversity of the Norfolk landscape. Edward VII loved the beauty of the pine forest, lonely heath, and arable land. Castle Rising has a Norman church as well as a historic fortress.

The level fenland landscape is an acquired taste. This is a walk on the banks of the rivers Wissey and Great Ouse to see Denver Sluice, the hub of the fen drainage system where three rivers meet.

Tracks, field paths, lanes and a former railway line feature in this walk. A highlight is the section through the park- and woodland at Little Dunham, a small estate typical of this part of central Norfolk.

Vast horizons open this walk, on a bank of the Great Ouse. There is a pub halfway and the return is on tracks, lanes and paths on the fringe where the fens begin to rise to the heights of west Norfolk.

One of the wonders of Norfolk is situated close to the vast village green at Hales. A small payment allows visitors to see the interior of the great barn, an amazing survivor.

After a stretch along a quiet lane the going is less easy, on the banks of the Yare and Chet. Hardley Flood, towards the end of the final leg, is a little-known haven for migrants and a variety of waterfowl.

Horsey Mere was the last habitat for the bittern. The blend of walking, over squelchy marshland and then on the yielding sand of Horsey beach, makes this short route memorable.

A mixture of field and riverside walking with a choice of pubs: the River Ant is a favourite waterway of the Broads, and the length between Ludham Bridge and How Hill provides a fair sample of its quality.

Once only rabbits provided a living for Breckland's inhabitants. The original landscape has all but disappeared though this walk takes in a surviving fragment. The return needs careful navigation.

Until the 1950s Thetford was a forgotten backwater of south Norfolk. The walk follows the river and then rights-of-way through Thetford Forest, where there is a section that may be muddy.

The upper valley of the River Bure is a particularly beautiful district. Mannington Hall, with its famous gardens, is regularly open to visitors in summer, while Wolterton is open less frequently.

This part of the River Nar's course is through agricultural land and woodland where you are unlikely to meet other walkers. The same goes for the woodland path through Marham Fen, a misleading name.

Felbrigg Hall is a Norfolk showpiece, as is the surrounding parkland. The National Trust keep the estate's footpaths in good condition. Elsewhere waymarking has been lost in a few places.

This walk entails a climb but it is a short and gentle ascent and there is a good view at the top. Overstrand is a shoreline village where the cliffs are unstable, with properties regularly being lost to the sea.

A visit to Oxborough Hall can be combined with this walk that gives a flavour of the surrounding countryside: pasture, forest, and vast fields for grain and sugar-beet. Gooderstone is a typical byway village.

The Peddars Way long-distance path provides excellent walking. It was probably in existence before the Romans arrived. Few Norfolk villages are as secluded as Fring.

This is a waymarked village walk showing signs of neglect but deserving to be better known. Both villages are pretty and have pubs and fine churches. The walk mainly uses field paths, some encroached.

The first part is a tribute to William Marriott, who brought railways to remote corners of Norfolk. The second half is mainly on beautiful green lanes that are little used and in danger of becoming choked.

The Ringland Hills is a beauty-spot loved by generations of Norwich people. It descends to the watermeadows by the River Wensum, perhaps wet. The return leg of the route becomes drier as you progress.

In Edwardian times a picnic at 'the Downs' was a highlight. Today this valley is a nature reserve and trees hide the small chalk quarries. The coastal part of the route will appeal to birdlovers.

This route takes you along the shore east of Wells and into rolling fields and attractive villages. The walk can start from Warham or Wighton at busy holiday times when car parks at Wells may be full.

The Little Ouse makes a fine start to this route that includes a medieval castle and goes close to the prehistoric flint mines at Grime's Graves. Nettles and, less commonly, adders may be encountered.

Access to the beautiful woods at Westwick is restricted to the bridleway. The walk starts at North Walsham Station, and there are frequent services from there to and from Norwich and Cromer.

This walk illustrates the character of the countryside of south Norfolk with its scattered farms and belts of trees obviously planted to meet the needs of shooting. Long Stratton is a village that is expanding rapidly.

Introduction
to Norfolk

Norfolk has never enjoyed much of a reputation for its scenery, Noël Coward famously dismissing it as 'Very flat, Norfolk' and Charles II as a place fit only to make roads for the rest of the kingdom. *White's Directory* to the county for 1883 says: 'The face of Norfolk may be considered as less varied in its features than that of any other tract of similar extent in this country'. I hope that anyone who manages to complete all twenty-eight walks in this book will realise that the truth is very different from these opinions. Ronald Blythe's comment that 'the scenery here carries undulation to the most subtle limits' hits the mark exactly.

The landscape

Norfolk's landscape owes its shape and features to comparatively recent events, most of them taking place at the end of the Ice Age, when retreating glaciers laid down their loads of gravel, sand and mud on a bedrock of chalk. In places the latter is close to the surface, overlain by thin deposits of sand. This gives the sandy heathlands in the north-west and south of the county, while elsewhere boulder clay deposited by the glaciers makes the fertile soil with which Norfolk farmers have been blessed.

The fenland in the far west of the county is a distinct region, shared with other counties. Much of it lies below mean sea-level, being drained by a complicated system of rivers, dykes and sluices. For more than 300 years this fertile land has depended on pumps for its existence, first powered by the wind, then by steam, diesel and now electricity. A similar landscape can be seen in the east of the county where the rivers Bure and Yare and their tributaries meander towards the sea, passing through lakes known hereabouts as broads. These are the result of man digging up deposits of peat to use for fuel, an activity that apparently went on from prehistoric until medieval times.

Norfolk's long coastline is rightly famous. Its fine, extensive beaches, crumbling cliffs and miles of sand-dunes alternate with shingle banks and salt-marshes through numerous coastal nature reserves.

Prehistory

About 10,000 years ago a group of travellers might have been seen on a Norfolk skyline on their way to trade for precious flakes of flint to tip their spears and arrows, and perhaps to help mine the flints from the deep chalk pits at Grimes Graves.

These Stone Age walkers used the track that wandered across the sandy upland of Norfolk and merged with the Icknield Way, which ended close to

Thatched houses in Pulham Market

Avebury. They looked at a virgin landscape where forest predominated and the only cleared land was on the heathy ridge grazed by aurochs (wild bison) and wild goats.

A fertile backwater
By the time the Romans came a small population was spread over the area, living in villages owing allegiance to a regional chief. The removal of trees had revealed that the soil of the land lying below the sandy ridges was highly fertile and provided rich pasture and tillage. The people here were the Iceni tribe. They initially supported the Romans, who were quick to set up lines of communication, forts and settlements throughout the region. Although Norfolk was a comparative backwater, it was bisected by one important road made in the early years of Roman occupation – today known as the Peddars Way – running from Thetford northwards to the shore of The Wash. However, within twenty years of the arrival of Roman garrisons, the Iceni under Queen Boudicca rose in revolt against the occupation. After early successes at Colchester and London the native tribe was comprehensively defeated by the vastly superior army. Boudicca took poison as the Romans set about annihilating her people. This was the only meaningful revolt against the Romans' rule and was a reason for their comparative neglect of the region.

Norman rule
When the next invading force arrived in 1066 after the defeat of King Harold at Hastings, they found Norfolk still sparsely populated. It had

suffered greatly in Anglo-Saxon times when Viking raids brought calamity to any town, village or monastery that appeared to be flourishing.

Norman rule brought stability and a social structure that was to last into the Tudor era. Serfs and peasants laboured for their overlords, and the peasants were granted strips of land to cultivate for themselves.

Sheep and churches

Gradually, as the Norman era came to an end, the felling of more and more trees transformed the landscape. Sheep were introduced to graze the rough pasture. In the 13th and 14th centuries new weaving techniques made Norfolk famous for the quality of its cloth. This generated huge wealth and much of it found its way to the Church, whose monasteries owned vast tracts of land. They used the windfall to extend their abbeys and priories while other landowners and many weavers invested spiritually, building churches in the hope of being assured of a place in heaven on the Day of Judgement.

Norfolk's incomparable legacy of country churches is largely due to the woollen boom, as are the fifty or so medieval churches in Norwich (the saying goes that within the city there is a church for every week of the year and a pub for every day – unhappily this is no longer true). In its medieval heyday Norwich was the third most prosperous city in England.

Rise of the yeoman farmer

The Black Death in the middle of the 14th century dealt a blow to economic expansion and caused the abandonment of many villages. Afterwards fortunes revived, and it is significant that the benefactors of churches began to be yeoman farmers who had come to be wealthy by working hard and marrying well rather than Anglo-Norman barons.

The end to the prosperity of the Church and the structure of medieval society was triggered by Henry VIII's dispute with Rome. The King dissolved the monasteries and in doing this removed the only safety net for the poor and sick apart from their landlords. His reign, and those of his two daughters brought great suffering to the nation as it seesawed between Protestantism and Catholicism.

Norfolk had martyrs from both camps who suffered horrible deaths. However, the latter part of Queen Elizabeth's reign saw the revival of prosperity and optimism. Many of the great families of the county – the Cokes, Walpoles and Townshends for example – laid down the foundation of their success at this time.

History wrought few changes to the landscape except that woodland continued to be cleared and towns and villages grew in tandem with an increasing population. Norfolk was fortunate in escaping the worst of the conflict during the Civil War, though some long-established Catholic families suffered greatly.

The agricultural revolutions

In the middle of the 18th century the Norfolk countryside began to be transformed after Thomas Coke of Holkham invented the four-course system of agriculture. This entailed a rotation system in fields where the grain harvest was followed by a crop of roots and then one of clover or vetch (sown in order to restore nitrogen). In the fourth year the land was left fallow. Cultivation following this pattern brought greatly improved yields and profits for landlords. However, it forced out tenant farmers who often could not pay increased rents. Furthermore, the landlords introduced another draconian measure for increasing their wealth by enclosing for themselves the common land where villagers had previously kept their livestock. At a stroke this did away with the livelihood of many common people and they were forced to quit their homes. The hardship caused by this was comparable to that of those evicted later in Ireland and Scotland. The result was the same: country people left either to work in the cities or emigrated to America and Australia.

By the end of the 19th century a new pattern was established. Fields were larger (though still only a quarter of the size of modern ones). Machines enabled farmers to make do with far fewer workers and so yet more cottages were abandoned. Tractors began to replace teams of horses after the First World War but the agricultural depression in the late 1920s stopped investment and forced many farmers from the land. Scottish farmers bought many of the holdings put up for sale at the time, and their

The entrance to Oxburgh Hall

descendants remain prominent landowners in Norfolk. Although the majority of the county's farmers continued to use horses into the 1950s, the appearance of more powerful tractors and combine harvesters made them redundant.

A new landscape

The new machinery meant that farmers grubbed up hedges to make large fields larger and better suited for mechanical cultivation. Workers left the land once more, quitting tied cottages their families had lived in for generations. These were eagerly bought by people who commuted into Norwich and the market towns.

Small farms were bought up by a handful of wealthy farmers who argued that the only way to make agriculture profitable was to operate large units.

When it was discovered that farming had become too efficient, creating vast surpluses of food, farmers began to be paid not to cultivate their fields, and 15 per cent now lies as 'setaside'. Responsible landowners make sure that this land remains beneficial to wildlife by sowing grasses and wild flowers, though others continue to spray weedkiller to leave the soil barren and probably poisonous. Anyone who has walked in Norfolk cannot fail to have noticed the steady diminution in wildlife. Sparrows, skylarks, ladybirds, honeybees, hares, hedgehogs and many insects are all becoming rare.

Public realisation is dawning at the scale of the loss of wildlife, and some remedies are appearing. Formerly public money was available to farmers if they pulled up hedgerows but now it is paid to replant them. More are creating havens for wildlife on the headlands of their fields, and many are turning to organic agriculture. However, many Norfolk farmers are tenants

The beach at Holme next the Sea

or are employed by financial institutions who pressure them to make profits. On the one hand some of them have to contend with low prices for their produce while on the other they are supposed to keep the footpaths over their land clear.

Practical walking in Norfolk

Horsey Dyke

'Bracing' is the usual description of Norfolk's climate, which means that it wakes you up in the morning and only chills if you stop walking briskly. On the other hand this is almost the driest part of Britain so a completely wet day is rare. However, Norfolk does seem to specialise in short, sharp showers that seem to come from nowhere, so it is advisable to carry a light rainproof unless you have trust in a sunny forecast.

In high summer, protection from the sun is vital, especially as many of these walks are over open countryside. A hat saves the head and face from direct sunshine, and if it has a peak or a brim it protects the eyes as well.

Be warned that it is inadvisable to walk any of these routes in shorts. Nettles make an appearance in early spring and by September are often head-high. Brambles and thistles also prey on unprotected flesh. If it has been dry for some days many of the walks can be tackled in walking-shoes or even in trainers but boots are recommended, both for the support they give to ankles and for keeping feet dry. If you start walking early in the morning the vegetation will be wet from dew and will test the moisture-resistant properties of any high-tech footwear. Long grass can hide deep ruts and puddles, and you may need luck and good balance as well as waterproof boots to cross flooded dykes and ditches, which are a common hazard in Norfolk.

Thetford Forest covers much of the south-west segment of the county and, thanks to the open-access policy of Forest Enterprise, provides a great deal of excellent walking. However, it is easy to become disoriented in the trees so it is as well to carry a compass to avoid navigational mistakes. Also, darkness falls early in the forest, and it is unnerving to have to tackle the last leg of a long walk in twilight or on a dull day when you cannot get direction even from the sun.

Wood Green from Long Stratton

Start	Public car park, Long Stratton
Distance	3 miles (4.8km)
Approximate time	1½ hours
Parking	Public car park behind the Angel Inn
Refreshments	Pubs and tearoom in Long Stratton
Ordnance Survey maps	Landranger 134 (Norwich & The Broads), Explorer 237 (Norwich)

Long Stratton has the Norwich to Ipswich road as its axis and has become an outflung suburb of the city with most modern developments being on the eastern side of the main road. In 1845 it was described as a market town, had only 690 inhabitants, but was still a busy staging post for coach traffic. The walk avoids the new housing, plunging straight into the countryside and then using grassy lanes and footpaths to make a short but attractive circuit.

From the car park walk to the main road, cross by the pedestrian crossing and turn left to pass the village sign and come to Star Lane **A**. Although marked as a cul-de-sac it leads to an enclosed footpath which runs below a high hedgerow to the right and a field to the left. Keep ahead when the path climbs to field level to walk on the left side of a field, heading for an old windmill almost concealed by modern grain silos and an old maltings. The landscape is flat and dotted with isolated cottages and houses. The path crosses three ditches and a stile before coming to a gate giving on to Mill Lane. Be careful if you climb the half-stile to the left – it would be easy to fall into the ditch!

Cross Mill Lane to the path on the other side and walk to the right of the hedge. Keep ahead at a footpath junction and cross another plank bridge on a pleasant footpath which joins Boudicca's Way at the corner of a wood **B**. Continue along the track that veers right at this point to skirt the wood. Morningthorpe church can be seen to the left beyond unsightly broiler houses. Cross Mill Road to the drive going to Mayfield Farm and pass the lovely old farmhouse. Keep ahead after this on a grassy track with the hedge to the right. At Wood Green leave Boudicca's Way by turning right on the track skirting the common to reach the road by the northern Wood Green Farm and turn right again.

After 150 yds (137m) leave the road to cross the ditch at a fingerpost **C** pointing across a large field (fortunately this path is cleared at most times of the year). The right of way makes a dog-leg in the middle of the field to reach Hall Lane close to a white cottage. Turn left

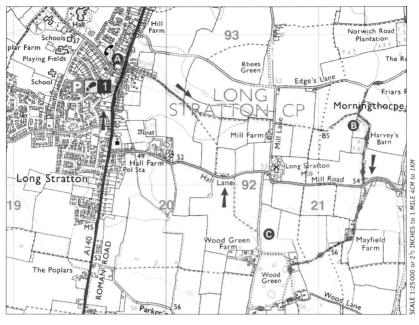

| 0 | 200 | 400 | 600 | 800 METRES | 1 |
| 0 | 200 | 400 | 600 YARDS | ½ |

KILOMETRES
MILES

to pass the cottage. Just before reaching the main road, look for a path to the right that goes through the churchyard to the main road. Long Stratton's round-towered church is dedicated to St Mary and dates from the 14th century. If you are fortunate enough to find it open you will see a Sexton's Wheel, used to choose the day of the

St Mary's Church, Long Stratton

Lady Fast, a movable fast-day which had to be observed for seven years. This is one of only two such instruments to survive, the other being at Yaxley in Suffolk.

Turn right along the main road from the churchyard and pass a row of shops. At the end of these are the remains of the ice-house that once served the manor-house, a 'handsome brick mansion on a slight eminence' demolished long ago. A short distance beyond this is the Angel Inn, and behind it is the car park where the walk began. ●

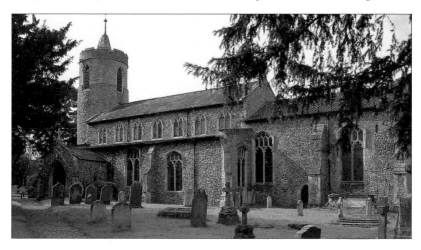

Ringland and the Wensum valley

Start	Ringland church
Distance	3 miles (4.8km)
Approximate time	1¼ hours
Parking	At church
Refreshments	Pub at Ringland
Ordnance Survey maps	Landranger 133 (North East Norfolk), Explorer 238 (East Dereham & Aylsham)

This short route is ideal as an evening stroll or to walk off the effects of a heavy Sunday lunch. It begins with an energetic climb, but after this the going is level. However, it will almost certainly be wet as well, especially across the meadows to the footbridge at Attlebridge Hall. There are also nettles and thistles.

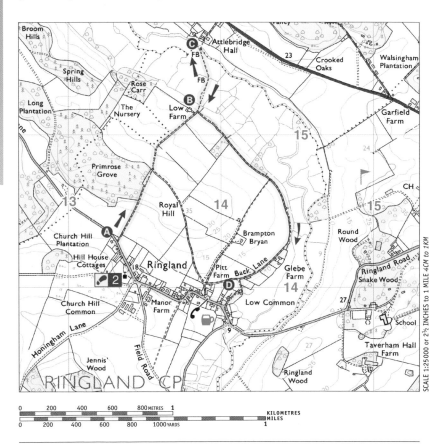

SCALE 1:25000 or 2½ INCHES to 1 MILE 4CM to 1KM

Footbridge over the River Wensum

If you get the opportunity, look inside Ringland church to see its splendid roof, comparable to that of St Peter Mancroft in Norwich. There is also some medieval stained glass.

✏ Walk past the east end of the church on the lane to Weston Longville, which was Parson Woodforde's village. He is most famous for his appetite, though his diaries also give other fascinating insights into the life of a Norfolk clergyman in the 18th century. He frequently visited Ringland.

Pass the Wesleyan chapel (now the village reading-room) and then turn right Ⓐ on to a track climbing to the edge of a wood. Keep ahead when another track joins from the right at the corner of the wood. There is a pleasant view over the well-wooded Wensum valley as the track descends to Low Farm.

Walk down the right-hand side of the fence around the farm to a stile Ⓑ. The path crosses an ancient brick bridge and crosses a meadow to a plank bridge.

Bear slightly left after this and walk across the next meadow (grazed by cattle in summer and likely to be waterlogged after wet weather) to the footbridge Ⓒ that spans the River Wensum in front of Attlebridge Hall, a lovely old farmhouse.

Return to Low Farm, cross the brick bridge but do not cross the stile at Ⓑ. Instead turn left and follow the hedge at the top of the field – the path sometimes encounters nettles and thistles here. Cross a stile to a path leading past the end of a copse. For a short way the path is broad and grassy but it soon becomes narrow again. After crossing two stiles at a field entrance, the right of way becomes a track running between high hedges and gradually swinging south-wards. Golfers on the far side of the river give the lovely view on the left a sense of scale. The going is now grassy again but soon reaches another track. Go left when this divides Ⓓ to reach the main road (the Swan Inn is to the left).

If you do not want refreshment turn right to walk along the main street of the village back to Ringland church. ●

Acle and Upton

Start	Acle Recreation Centre
Distance	4½ miles (7.2km)
Approximate time	2 hours
Parking	At start
Refreshments	Pubs at Acle, Upton and Acle Bridge
Ordnance Survey maps	Landranger 134 (Norwich & The Broads), Explorer OL40 (The Broads)

The village of Acle is situated close between the two river systems of the Broads: the Bure and its tributaries to the north, the rivers Yare and Waveney to the south. The walk begins by using the ancient field path that runs from Acle to the quiet village of Upton, passing the disused round-towered church at Fishley. After walking through Upton, the route follows a footpath skirting the marshes to reach another on the bank of the River Bure that eventually leads back to Acle. Note that Acle holds a busy market on Thursdays. The walk can start from Upton staithe or Acle Bridge if the car park at Acle is full.

📝 Walk out of the car park past the library and Methodist church and turn right. After 100 yds (91m) turn right again down Pyebush Lane and bear left at the cemetery **Ⓐ** on to a short track which soon becomes a field path leading past a pillbox. The churches at Upton and Fishley are prominent in the wide, if rather featureless, landscape. The latter little church is surrounded by trees and has a round tower built of flints. It is rewarding to visit the peaceful churchyard even though the church is locked.

The footpath continues ahead past the churchyard **Ⓑ** over a large field. It is well used and is usually cleared and rolled. It crosses the next, smaller,

field in the same direction and comes to an enclosed path leading into Upton. Turn right at the road and then immediately left into the Green. At Boat Dyke Road keep ahead for 100 yds (91m) if you wish to visit the pub, the White Horse, otherwise turn right to continue down Boat Dyke Road.

The Norfolk wherry Albion

Bear right at the junction with Back Lane and walk through the car park at the staithe and then up the right-hand side of the dyke. After 50 yds (46m) turn right **C** on a footpath running between the ditch and a wood. This leads into carr (scrubland with many elder trees) with a ditch to each side. This, in turn, takes you to open marshland. Birdwatchers will find that the reedbeds here are excellent habitats for reed and sedge warblers while heron will be seen watching open water for prey. A glance at the map shows that Rattlesnake Carr is not far from the path, and it is puzzling to think why that patch of scrub to the south of Fishley Hall came by that name.

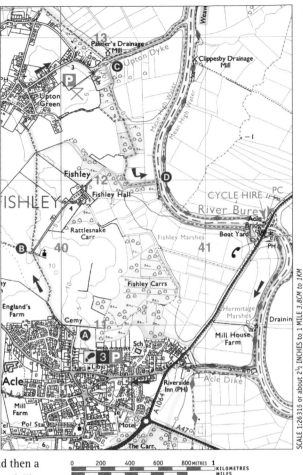

SCALE 1:26315 or about 2½ INCHES to 1 MILE 3.8CM to 1KM

0	200	400	600	800 METRES	1
					KILOMETRES
					MILES
0	200	400	600 YARDS	½	

The path crosses a track and then a metal footbridge to enter a wood. The river is close at hand when the path emerges to cross a succession of stiles and then run down the side of a belt of trees. It reaches the river **D** at a sailing club. Turn right to walk along the bank.

The River Bure is the busiest of the Broadland rivers and there is amusement in watching the boats and their crews if the traffic is heavy. Walking on the grassy banktop is pleasant, and it is not long before the boatyards at Acle Bridge come into view. The footpath leaves the riverbank and follows a roadway through the boatyards to the road. Take care in crossing the road to the entrance to the Bridge Inn. Then, if not taking refreshment, continue past the pub with its circular thatched extension (the main part of the pub is

old). Note that the footpath runs a few yards inland after the pub garden for a short distance before rejoining the riverbank. The waymarks bear the Weavers Way badge, a long-distance footpath that runs from Great Yarmouth to Cromer.

At Acle Dike the path is forced to turn away from the river and a fence separates it from the boatyard by the dyke. At the head of the dyke the Weavers Way leaves to the left to continue by the river. Instead cross the road and turn left, and then keep ahead to take the road into Acle past the East Norwich Inn (The Cabin) and the fire station. Fork right on the road to return to the starting point. ●

Northrepps from Overstrand

Start	Overstrand
Distance	4 miles (6.4km)
Approximate time	2 hours
Parking	Clifftop car park in summer. On-street parking in village in winter
Refreshments	Pubs at Overstrand and Northrepps
Ordnance Survey maps	Landranger 133 (North East Norfolk), Explorer 252 (Norfolk Coast East)

The cliffs to the east of Cromer are notoriously unstable and the village of Overstrand is under constant threat as the sea worries at its shoreline. The power of erosion is well seen on the final part of this route, which also visits an attractive north Norfolk village, using quiet lanes and farm tracks.

Turn right from the car park and follow the lane for about ¼ mile (400m) before turning left immediately after Arden Close 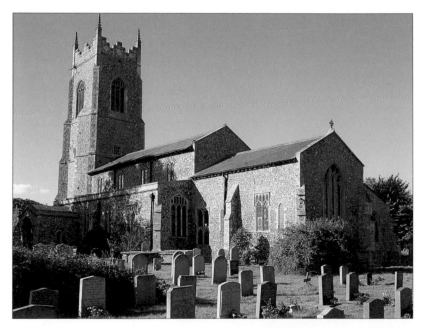 on to an enclosed footpath which takes you up to the main road. Cross this to a private road almost opposite with a circular walk logo on the gatepost. This becomes a pleasant, enclosed track climbing to cross the obsolete railway line which once ran along the coast from Cromer to Great Yarmouth. Overstrand station

Northrepps church

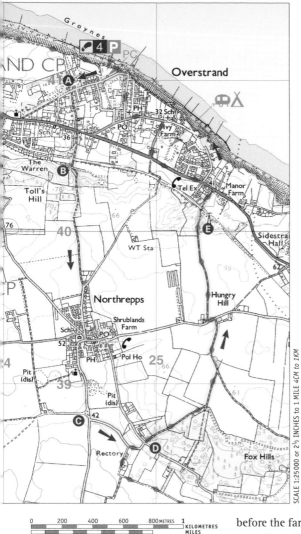

left at the impressive rectory to join the Paston Way, a 20-mile (32km) route from North Walsham to Cromer that celebrates north Norfolk's best-known medieval family, whose letters illuminate the domestic and political life of a powerful family at the time of the Wars of the Roses.

At a T-junction **D** keep ahead on to a footpath climbing towards a wood and passing three massive oak trees on the right. At the top of the hill the footpath emerges from the wood and there is open countryside to the left. As it swings away from the wood the way is likely to be muddy after wet weather, as it is further on after another track joins from the right. At Hungry Hill turn left at the lane and walk a few yards and then,

before the farm, turn right on to a field track that ultimately leads to a radar installation. Just before reaching this, however, leave by keeping ahead **E** on to a footpath, bearing the Paston Way logo, that descends to the main road.

Turn left but after 50 yds (45m) leave the main road to the right on a road where a sign says that there is no vehicular access to the beach. When this road swings away from the badly eroded clifftop take the tarmac drive down to the promenade. The unstable nature of the cliffs is well illustrated as you walk back to Overstrand where, after about ½ mile (800m), a zigzag driveway climbs the cliffs to a point close to the starting point. ●

was to the right. After this, take the footpath to the right **B** after the track swings left to serve the allotments. At the top the path joins a field track leading towards Northrepps church.

Keep ahead to the village centre and pass the former village school before turning right down Church Street – the village pub is a few steps to the left from this corner. Just before the church the Parsons Pleasure Hotel offers an alternative venue for refreshment. Continue along the lane after the church until you come to a 'Quiet Lane' on the left **C**. Take this byway, bearing

The two Pulhams

Start	Pulham Market
Distance	4½ miles (7.2km)
Approximate time	2 hours
Parking	Small car park in Falcon Road at the centre of the village
Refreshments	Pubs at Pulham Market and Pulham St Mary
Ordnance Survey maps	Landranger 156 (Saxmundham), Explorer 230 (Diss & Harleston)

This is a fairly short but enjoyable route linking two south Norfolk villages that were prosperous in medieval times. This is reflected in the beauty of their churches. The paths are mainly on the edges of fields, and nettles may be a problem in places.

Pulham Market was granted a market charter in 1249 but declined in the 18th century and failed to revive even when connected by railway. The large church, dedicated to St Mary Magdalen, reflects the time when the village was at the peak of its fortune. The beautiful Market Green is overlooked by two pubs and pretty thatched cottages.

From the car park turn left, cross the main road and then turn right down a lane. After 25 yds (23m) turn left down a track, following a sign to the Bowls Club and a waymark. After the entrance to the Bowls Club go down the enclosed footpath to the left at the gateway ahead. After crossing a plank bridge, open countryside faces you on a field-edge path heading towards a prefabricated building. However, after 100 yds (91m) turn right **A** and walk along the edge of the field, whose headland is in danger of being choked by brambles and nettles. Turn right at the end of the ditch and walk into a thicket where, within yards, there is a waymark at present overgrown by vegetation. The path goes through the spinney,

passing a planting of young trees to the right and crossing a deep ditch where it enters more woodland before crossing a narrow field to reach a lane. Turn left.

The lane climbs to the dizzy height of 174ft (53m) and there is an excellent view to the south. At a T-junction go right and after walking 50 yds (46m) leave the lane to the left **B** on a field-edge path that follows a ditch around a vast field. You will be a lonely figure in this hedgeless agricultural prairie as you walk along the side of the deep ditch. Two footpaths go to the left, crossing the ditch, but there are no bridges across the obstacle.

When faced by a ditch ahead, turn right **C** to walk along it to North Farm. Turn right along the lane for 50 yds (46m) and then leave it on a greenway that heads towards a red-brick cottage. Turn right at the lane and walk towards the tower of Pulham St Mary church in the distance. Pass Church Farm and a modern bungalow and go through the opening to the left after this (there is no waymark) and walk by the side of the property before crossing the field to a

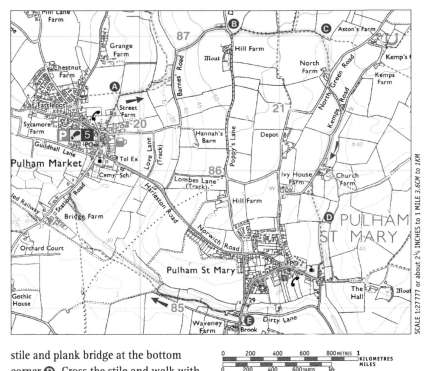

SCALE 1:27777 or about 2¼ INCHES to 1 MILE 3.6CM to 1KM

stile and plank bridge at the bottom corner **D**. Cross the stile and walk with the hedge to the right to come to another stile. After this the path may be threatened by brambles and nettles but it should still be possible to reach the churchyard at Pulham St Mary.

This church is notable for its porch, lavishly decorated with shields and figures, amongst the latter eight music-making angels. The dedication of the church here is to St Mary the Virgin, but it still must have been confusing for Pulham villagers to have both churches called St Mary's!

Turn right at the road and at the King's Head turn left down Station Road. The village sign shows airships which were based here during the First World War and subsequently. The former school is on the corner here. It looks like a normal Victorian structure but as you walk past it you will see the old windows and masonry of a much earlier building. Originally the medieval guild chapel of St James, it was adapted into a schoolroom founded by William Pennoyer in 1670.

0	200	400	600	800 METRES	1
					KILOMETRES
					MILES
0	200	400	600 YARDS	½	

Keep ahead on Station Road when another road joins and cross a bridge. Turn right after Willowburn **E** (no waymark) on a grassy track leading to an iron gate. The path goes to the left to another iron gate, which you will have to climb. A long meadow follows and, though it may be tempting to follow the bank of the stream, it is advisable to keep to the left to find a track along the old railway line, which takes you into another meadow and then to a high stile becoming smothered by undergrowth. There is a footpath junction after the stile. Turn right and then left before a bridge (waymark defaced) to walk on a grassy field-edge track. Cross a metal-plank bridge and continue ahead with the ditch to the right. Turn right to cross a bridge by an ash tree. The nettles may be a problem on the other side, and after the path turns left to enter a green lane, though here there is a supply of dock leaves. Turn right at Station Road to return to the centre of the village. ●

Horsey

Start	Horsey drainage mill (on B1159)
Distance	5 miles (8km)
Approximate time	2 hours
Parking	National Trust Pay and Display car park at Horsey Staithe (National Trust members should get free ticket from shop and display it behind windscreen)
Refreshments	Pub in Horsey, seasonal lunch/tearoom at Delph Farm
Ordnance Survey maps	Landranger 134 (Norwich & The Broads), Explorer OL40 (The Broads)

No other walk illustrates the unique appeal of Broadland as well as this circuit, which also takes in a particularly unspoilt stretch of Norfolk's coastline. Be warned that the going may be difficult if the weather has been wet, and sections may be moist even after several days without rain. Bird lovers will appreciate the opening section through reedbeds on the fringe of the mere, while children will love the sandy beach that follows. Few people will fail to enjoy the hospitality of the Nelson Head ❻, a pub owned by the National Trust. Note that the path through the meadows from the Nelson Head to the staithe is not a right of way and is closed from November to February inclusive.

🥾 Take the footpath from the toilet block and walk up the north side of the dyke, away from the mill. The path swings right before coming to the mere but there are views of it over the reedbeds. The thatched boathouse on the left is a reminder that this was once a prized venue with wildfowlers. Pochard and goldeneye teal may be seen on the water with slightly more common birds like great crested grebe. Reed bunting and sedge warblers are to be seen flitting through the reeds, though the bearded tit is the species which every 'twitcher' seeks. Rarest of all Broadland birds is the bittern, only a few pairs surviving in the deepest reedbeds. Their distinctive mating call, like a foghorn, was once a feature of places like Horsey.

The path leaves the fringes of the mere and crosses a plank bridge to reach a stile ❹ giving on to a meadow. (However, follow the indicated Broads Authority footpath, which may be diverted from right of way for conservation reasons). Cross the field to a stile standing on the other side by a post bearing a black board with a white disc. The path soon meets the side of a dyke – Waxham New Cut – and turns right to head northwards.

The way along the bank of the dyke is narrow and may be waterlogged in places. People are asked not to stand in groups here as this disturbs the birdlife. Herons are common but marsh harriers, the largest bird of prey on the Broads, are rarely seen. Both hunt the natterjack toad, a threatened species which frequents the pastures behind the sand dunes (still known as the warren).

The path turns right at Brograve Mill **B**, a ruined drainage mill replaced by the electric pump standing close by, and runs along the edge of a field. It swings left and then right to skirt the small wood in front and come to a lane. Go right and then immediately left here to follow a field path on the left-hand edge of a field. At a T-junction **C** turn left on another field-edge path, leading to the coast road.

*For the shorter route, turn right on to a footpath that leads to a lane going past the church. Fork left when the lane divides to reach the main road and then go ahead for 200 yds (183m) to a telephone box. Keep ahead here to reach the Nelson Head **F**.*

Turn right along the road for 100 yds (91m) to come to a sharp bend **D**. Turn left here to head towards the sea down a broad track (or detour right for refreshments at Delph Farm). The sand dunes ahead, with their covering of marram grass, are all that protect the shoreline parishes from inundation, a fate that befell them when Horsey Gap was breached in 1953. The right of way runs southeastwards behind the dunes, but if the weather is favourable you may prefer to walk along the beach which, out of season, is often deserted. If the tide is out beyond the groynes beware of being stranded on the seaward side of the deep lagoon – the tide comes in remarkably quickly on this coast. Note

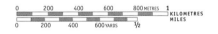

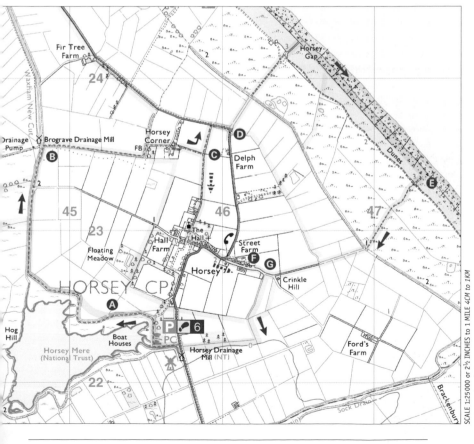

the exposed blue clay where the sea has scoured away the sand. The drop on the southeastern side of the groynes shows the direction the sand is travelling.

The seaside walk extends to about ¾ mile (1.2km) but the soft sand makes the going difficult so it may take 40 minutes or so. Look for steps up the sea wall but do not climb them. Instead go through the gap **E** and cross the footpath (unless you have taken it to avoid being exposed to a wind off the sea, in which case turn right) to walk along an inviting green lane. There may be deep puddles on this leg of the walk if there has been recent wet weather.

A hard surface is reached at Crinkle Hill. Bear right on to this for a short way to reach the Nelson Head **F**. The pub is situated 100 yds (91m) beyond a permissive path on the left marked with a National Trust badge on a post **G**, which provides an excellent way of returning to Horsey Staithe. However, the path is closed between November to February inclusive, when the road will have to be used instead.

At first the permissive path is a reed-fringed grassy track that in winter gives views of Horsey Mill behind trees and, in contrast, wind generators on the skyline. When the grassy track ends turn left. Climb the stile in front and turn right towards the windmill to walk by the side of a dyke past a small wood to return to the starting point.

The remains of Brograve Drainage Mill

Hales Green from Loddon

Start	Church Plain, Loddon
Distance	5 miles (8km)
Approximate time	2 hours
Parking	At start
Refreshments	Pubs and cafés at Loddon
Ordnance Survey maps	Landranger 134 (Norwich & The Broads), Explorer OL40 (The Broads)

The outward part of the route uses the Hobart Way, a circular route celebrating an ancient local family – one of them gave his name to the city of Hobart in Australia. The Hobarts used to inhabit Hales Hall but only the gatehouse of their 15th-century mansion survives, with a wonderful barn of the same date, the largest in Norfolk.

'Loddon', says a directory of 1845, 'is a small but pleasant market town, consisting chiefly of one long street, on the summit and acclivities of an eminence'. Its 19th-century pretensions are reflected in its little town hall and the building that now houses the library but was originally built as a school in 1857. In the first edition of *Buildings of England* in 1962 this was described as 'shocking' but by the time of the second edition (1999) the description had mellowed to 'amusing' – a good example of how we have come to accept Victorian eccentricity. Both town hall and library overlook Church Plain, which serves as a car park.

✐ Walk up to the south porch of the church, which dates from the 15th century but was drastically restored between 1870 and 1900. The south porch is its outstanding feature. It has two storeys – the upper one housing a local history exhibition – and is elaborately decorated. The church is dedicated to the Holy Trinity, whose figures are shown above the entrance,

sheltered by a vaulted canopy.

Turn away from the porch and walk across the churchyard on a narrow gravel path, which leads into an enclosed way that allows glimpses of water meadows to the left. Go left at the road, pass Low Bungay Road on the right, and gently descend to a bridge. On the far side of this turn right **Ⓐ** on to a grassy path with a ditch to the right. This is a pleasant shady way to the main road, though there are factories close by to the left, screened by trees.

Cross the main road to a kissing-gate almost opposite and walk through a meadow that has a mini-escarpment to the left (Warren Hills, still the home to hundreds of rabbits). Keep close to this sandy cliff to find a stile in the left corner of the meadow **Ⓑ**. Turn left here to climb a path enclosed by tall hedges. Turn left before the converted barn at Loddon Hall and then bear right to skirt the property. Climb a stile to reach the third side and go right again to walk by a hedge with a pond on the other side. There is a cricket ground to the left.

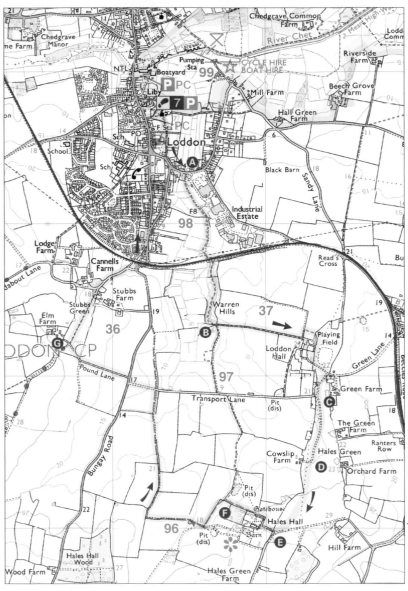

SCALE 1:25000 or 2½ INCHES to 1 MILE 4CM to 1KM

0   200   400   600   800 METRES   1
                                        KILOMETRES
                                        MILES
0   200   400   600 YARDS   ½

Cross the drive going to the hall and walk on for a short way with a wood to the right to pass a house and reach a gravel track. Bear right on to this, pass the end of Transport Lane on the right **C** and a South Norfolk Council notice declaring the track to be private. However, this does not apply to walkers,

who have the right to cross the wide and beautiful Hales Green, which is common land. The track passes several former farms before swinging right to the last of them, Cowslip Farm, newly rebuilt in bright red brick.

Leave the track here **D** to walk across the common – you will see a grassy track that is thistle-free, taking you to the corner **E** nearest to Hales Hall. Turn right to go through the gate

Holy Trinity Church, Loddon

by the cattle-grid – it is worth walking through the car park to view the magnificent 15th-century barn, and for a small charge you can see its interior as well.

However, this is a detour from the route. Keep ahead down the drive and bear right to walk round the outside. Only the gatehouse and one range survive of the great house built by Sir James Hobart *c*. 1470. He was subsequently King Henry VII's Attorney General. Pass the hall and continue on a

The 15th-century barn at Hales

bridleway with a wood to the left. Turn left after the wood **F** and then right at a T-junction. After this keep ahead on a field-edge bridleway heading west. Turn right at the end of the field. At the end of the following field the right of way goes through a tunnel of high hedges for a short way before it resumes as a field-edge track. Turn left when this meets a lane.

At a road, turn right and then left into Pound Lane, heading for Stubbs Green. Where the road divides to Bush Farm and Elm Farm, go through the ancient kissing-gate to the right **G**. Head across the field, aiming for the bottom right-hand corner where there is another kissing-gate. Go through this and keep ahead to reach a lane which takes you to the Bungay road. Turn left, cross the main road, and then keep ahead down High Bungay Road to return to the town centre and the starting point. ●

Oxborough and Gooderstone

Start	Oxborough
Distance	5 miles (8km)
Approximate time	2 hours
Parking	At village centre
Refreshments	Pubs at Oxborough and Gooderstone. Tearoom at Oxburgh Hall in season
Ordnance Survey maps	Landranger 143 (Ely & Wisbech), Explorer 236 (King's Lynn, Downham Market & Swaffham)

This is a short, level walk which illustrates many aspects of rural life in west Norfolk. Farm tracks are mainly used for the outward leg while a footpath through meadows and along fields makes up the return from Gooderstone.

Oxburgh Hall (the hall is spelt differently from the village) has been the home of the Bedingfeld family since the 15th century, a well-fortified manor house standing square within a moat. The magnificent gatehouse tower dates from around 1482 and its first-floor chamber was occupied by King Henry VII when he visited in 1487. However, in the 18th century the Tudor building had become ramshackle so the range opposite the gatehouse, which contained the great hall, was pulled down. Fortunately, the sixth baronet rebuilt the wing and restored the rest of the house in a sympathetic way in Victorian times, guided by an up-and-coming young architect, A.W.N. Pugin.

Oxborough village church is hardly less remarkable or romantic. Until 1948 it stood intact, its tower topped by one of the highest spires in the county. This suddenly fell, demolishing most of the church with the exception of the beautiful Bedingfeld Chapel at the end of the south aisle and all of the north aisle. The latter now serves as the parish church.

📐 Walk past the east end of the church and across the green to take the road heading north-west towards Eastmoor. A footpath leaves the road to the right but, since the going may be tricky on this path over cultivated fields, continue a little further to a bridleway (the waymark is on the opposite side of the road). You may think the footpath a little further on, which crosses Caldecote Fen, looks more inviting, but this crosses a meadow grazed by cattle with a bull in summer and traverses a vast field where, again, the walking may be uncomfortable. Thus it is recommended that you turn right along the farm track opposite the waymark **Ⓐ** which winds pleasantly between fields heading towards woodland. Turn left **Ⓑ** at a T-junction to pass through a small wood. The track is now heading north until just before it meets the road at Caldecote Farm. Turn right.

It is hard to find any sign of St Mary's Church which, according to the map, once stood opposite the barn. Walk along the lane, which gives views over

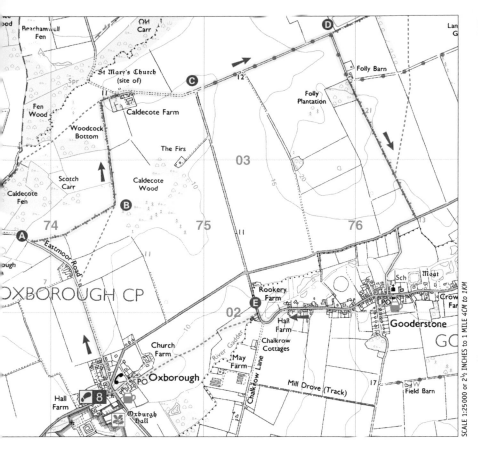

SCALE 1:25000 or 2½ INCHES to 1 MILE 4CM to 1KM

fields almost as unending as those in the American Midwest. All hedgerows have gone here, only a few isolated oak trees are left standing to remind us that before prairie-style agriculture this was a countryside of small fields encompassed by hedgerows teeming with wildlife.

Keep ahead on a sandy track when the lane turns right **C**. Now there are hedges, but strangely the brambles fail to yield blackberries. When you see the tall banks of a reservoir ahead and to the left, follow the major track to the right **D**. Pass Folly Barn (now a residence) and Folly Plantation. Twisted Scots' pines are a notable ingredient of the landscape here. They are the indigenous tree of Breckland and the other sandy heaths of Norfolk.

Turn right at the road and then take the lane to the left into Gooderstone

village, passing the 13th-century church. The Swan Inn is just to the left as you come to the main street.

Turn right and walk past a typical blend of rural properties, old and new. The road bends sharply just before Chalkrow Lane. Keep on it to cross the tiny River Gadder and then turn left **E** after the waterworks, climbing a stile to enter a meadow.

Pass a metal gate on the left and then bear right to the far right-hand corner of the field, where there is a stile. A grassy field-edge path lies beyond. Just before the end of a field, a stile on the right gives on to a short length of enclosed path. Turn left at the end of this to reach the inn and church at Oxborough. ●

Metton and Felbrigg Park

Start	Felbrigg Park
Distance	5½ miles (8.9km). Shorter version 4 miles (6.4km)
Approximate time	2½ hours (2 hours for shorter version)
Parking	National Trust car park at Felbrigg Hall
Refreshments	Tearoom at Felbrigg Hall in season (closed Thursdays)
Ordnance Survey maps	Landranger 133 (North East Norfolk), Explorer 252 (Norfolk Coast East)

The National Trust has excellent waymarked walks within Felbrigg Park and these would take the best part of a day to explore, but this one is offered as an alternative and explores the countryside to the south of Felbrigg. The Weavers Way has been rerouted here but the rights of way it used before survive, and are used for the outward leg. The return is on the new Weavers Way – the walker may decide whether this is an improvement.

Felbrigg Hall was built by Thomas Windham in 1621, which gives it almost exactly the same date as Blickling Hall, only seven miles (11.3km) away. Many of the craftsmen and decorators probably worked at both houses, and certainly Felbrigg shares many architectural features with Blickling. The west wing was added in 1675, and further alterations and additions took place in the 18th and 19th centuries. Repton was consulted in 1793 but it is not known whether he influenced the scheme of things. It seems unlikely since by this time the multitude of trees planted by William Windham between 1673 and 1687 would have reached maturity.

🖉 Follow the gravel path to the church from the end of the car park nearest the hall. Be sure to visit the church, which has box pews and outstanding monuments and brasses. The earliest brass is that of Simon de Felbrigg who died in 1351. A later one shows another Sir Simon with his first wife Margaret (d. 1416). She was cousin and maid of honour to Anne of Bohemia, queen of Richard II, and was herself a princess.

Leave the churchyard by the small gate in its northeast corner, immediately pass through a second gate and turn right to walk east across the meadow heading for a small gate on the far side **A**. Turn right on to the farm track and keep ahead at a crossways on a path that crosses a field towards trees. It goes into the trees and then turns sharply right to reach another crossways. Cross straight over the track and walk down the edge of the field with a wood to the right. When this ends **B** the right of way continues southwards across the field, heading to the left of electricity poles and the chimney of a house beyond. A pair of stiles will be found by an oak tree. Climb these and then bear left to pass a waymark in the middle of the field that points to another stile and a plank bridge. From this the path leads directly to Metton church. Note the passageway passing

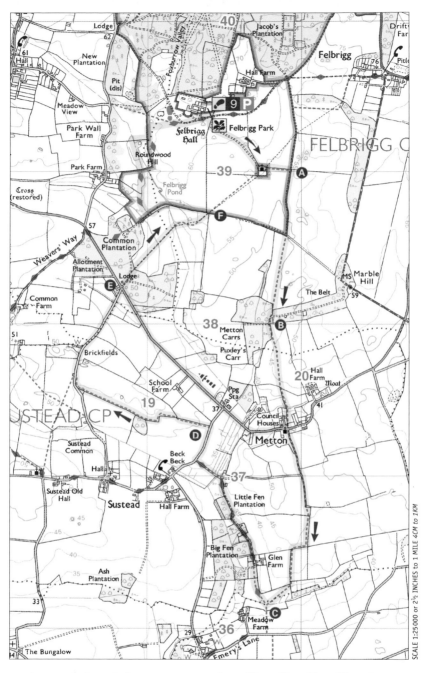

SCALE 1:25 000 or 2½ INCHES to 1 MILE 4CM to 1KM

| 0 | 200 | 400 | 600 | 800 METRES | 1 |
| 0 | 200 | 400 | 600 YARDS | ½ | KILOMETRES MILES |

north to south through the tower which allowed processions to stay on consecrated ground.

Cross the road to the track running past the east side of the churchyard.

Alternatively, turn right along the road to reach the south lodge for the shorter version of the walk.

The track swings left and right and then becomes a field-edge path with the hedge to the left. Turn right at the end of the field, following the direction shown on a white-topped post. After

Felbrigg Hall

about 150 yds (137m) steps on the left lead down to a field, and there is a Weavers Way signpost directing walkers along the right-hand edge of a field. After a stile at the bottom, turn right to walk along the top of a meadow with the hedge to the right. The new version of the Weavers Way is joined at a waymark standing by a young ash tree.

Continue on the path by the hedge and at a corner where there is another waymark **C**, turn northwards, still with the hedge to the right. Cross a stile and within a short distance join a concrete drive at Glen Farm, passing a car park for anglers who fish in the pond here. A pleasant leafy track leads to a lane at a place called Beck Beck. Leave Weavers' Lane by turning right here.

After 300 yds (274m) turn left **D** on to a footpath that crosses a plank bridge and runs along the edge of a field past a storm-shattered ash tree, the only remains of the hedgerow. At the end of the field the path bends left and right to reach a small wood. After running along the edge of this, the right of way carries on to a field corner where it bears right for a short way before emerging on to a lane.

Turn right along the quiet byway, noting that it is a designated Roadside Nature Reserve. At the end of the lane, cross a road and walk past the lodge into the park.

The shorter route joins here.

When the drive swings left, leave it at the end of the bend **E**, turning right on to a short grassy path leading to a stile. Head towards the church, descending to an opening at the bottom where the ground is moist. Bear slightly to the left from here to climb to a path running by the side of a wall. Turn sharply left here (by a seat) **F** and follow the wall, and then a fence, to Felbrigg Pond.

The route follows the Weavers Way and a mauve waymark around the shore of the pond and over a long boardwalk. Climb up after this and then leave the Weavers Way, keeping ahead through a gate into parkland when the enclosed path bends left. Head for the trees to the left of the hall to find a metal gate giving on to the main drive. Turn right to head back to the car park. ●

Marham Fen and the Nar Valley Way

Start	Narborough
Distance	5½ miles (8.9km)
Approximate time	2½ hours
Parking	At start in the cul-de-sac behind the bus shelter at the end of Narford Road
Refreshments	Pub at Narborough
Ordnance Survey maps	Landranger 143 (Ely & Wisbech), Explorer 236 (King's Lynn, Downham Market & Swaffham)

Only short lengths of road are used on this route, at the beginning and end at Narborough. For the rest of the time the walker is on footpaths, woodland tracks, and on the riverbank of the lovely River Nar. This is one of the best sections of the Nar Valley Way, and having sampled it here many will be encouraged to try other lengths, either downstream to King's Lynn or towards the source at Gressenhall.

Swans on the River Nar

✏️ Cross the main road and keep ahead into Denny's Walk (also known as Meadow Close at this end). Keep ahead into Meadow Road when the major road swings right, and keep ahead too when a lane leaves to the left and a footpath joins on the right. About 50 yds (46m) before the track ends at a gate go left **A** across a field following a bridleway waymark to a belt of conifers. Pass through this and keep ahead past two groups of oak trees to come to a farm track. Continue ahead, crossing a bridge by an electricity post and coming at last to a concrete track. Turn left and then right following a track on the edge of woodland. Cross another track and go through a metal gate into Marham Fen **B**.

Marham Fen was originally cut by the people of the village for wood and fodder. It is now managed by Anglian Water with the involvement of the Norfolk Wildlife Trust and the British Trust for Conservation Volunteers. The fen has a range of habitats. The woodland is noted for its butterfly species, and the open grassland supports a variety of flora and insect life.

A delightful woodland walk follows on a good track. Turn right at a T-junction **C** away from Marham (now a village with no pubs – once it had four of them). The route now strikes north east across Marham Fen where occasional patches of reed show that this wetland is a rare survival of natural fen.

At the end of the wood, cross over a farm track to a broader one ahead and walk down towards a pumping station that stands by the River Nar. Turn right here **D** to walk with the river to the left. The walking is somewhat more difficult now, grass hiding ruts made by tractors. The sound of rushing water heralds a weir where a large waterwheel stands in a state of decay.

Almost too soon Narborough church appears to the right and the roofs of the bungalows that house most of the inhabitants of the village. Near to the road the way ahead is blocked by a garden, and there is a detour via a narrow path leading into a cul-de-sac. Turn right to the main road. The Ship Inn is to the left, just a few steps away on the other side of the Nar.

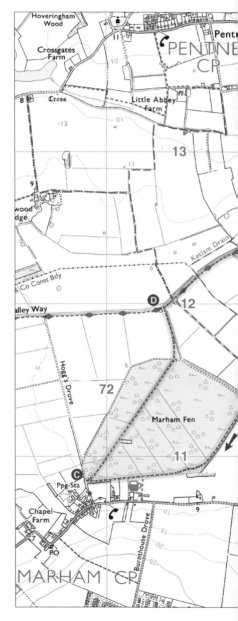

Narborough had two working watermills until recently but now both have been put to other purposes. Narborough Mill was built around 1780, is now a listed building and still contains its machinery. It is three storeys high and brick-built with a pantiled roof. Charles Tyssen enlarged it with an extension in 1845 but this was not well-built and the foundations sank slowly over time

causing part of the roof to collapse in 1980. This whole section, together with the Victorian miller's house on the front had to be demolished.

Turn right to return to the starting point, passing the church (which has a Norman nave) on the right. ●

Great Fransham and Little Dunham

Start	Great Fransham church
Distance	6 miles (9.7km)
Approximate time	2½ hours
Parking	On road close to Great Fransham church
Refreshments	Pub at Little Dunham
Ordnance Survey maps	Landranger 132 (North West Norfolk), Explorer 238 (East Dereham & Aylsham)

This undemanding circuit takes in landscapes typical of central Norfolk, using bridleways and quiet lanes as well as a drive passing through mature parkland. Little Dunham has a beautiful parish church and a pub that marks the walk's half-way point.

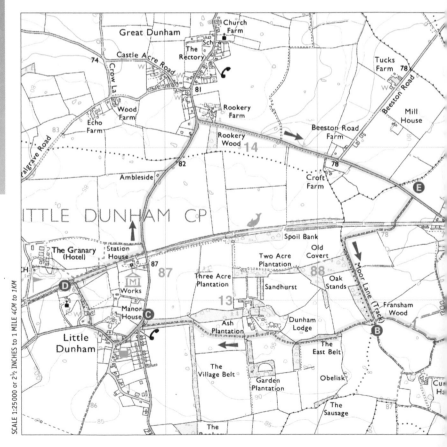

SCALE 1:25000 or 2½ INCHES to 1 MILE 4CM to 1KM

It is usually possible to park opposite the church at Great Fransham but there are also other places to park further up the lane.

🖉 Walk northwards from the church (that is with the church to the right) and at the junction turn left on to a farm track **A** that is likely to be muddy if it has recently been used by horses. At this point the track is a bridleway, but horses also make use of some of the footpaths encountered further on. The track runs through open farmland with the isolated Field House Farm to the right. Bear right when the track divides to follow the side of a ditch winding towards a wood. In winter you will catch a glimpse of

Dunham Lodge ahead before the bridleway meets Moor Lane **B**.

Keep ahead to cross this ancient green way and continue following the track when it bends left to avoid the Lodge. It passes through a belt of trees and joins the drive coming from the house, built in 1784–5.

The parkland, with its venerable oak trees, is delightful and must be at the peak of its beauty today, with some of the oaks being two centuries old.

At the park gates **C** cross the road to enter Little Dunham.

Opposite the Black Swan bear right to walk down Sporle Road, turning right at the Old School House, just before the bend, down School Lane. At the old railway line, turn right **D** to walk below the embankment. When the latter ends, the walker will feel rather exposed to golfers whose tees and fairways seem perilously close. At the end of the golf course the footpath crosses to the other side of the line and reaches the road.

This was once the site of Dunham station, which handled about six stopping trains in each direction between King's Lynn and Dereham at the height of its prosperity.

Turn left on to the road and follow it to Great Dunham but, before entering the village, turn right towards Great Fransham on an even quieter lane. After about 1 mile (1.6km), at the Great Fransham village sign, turn right **E** to join a farm track that crosses the railway over a bridge. The track soon becomes Moor Lane, which is a footpath unfortunately often used by horse-riders and thus likely to be muddy in places, especially where it passes through Fransham Wood.

Turn left at the crossways **B** to pass Field House Farm again and so return to Great Fransham church back at the starting point. ●

How Hill and Ludham

Start	How Hill, near Ludham
Distance	5½ miles (8.9km)
Approximate time	2½ hours
Parking	Car park for Toad Hole Cottage, How Hill
Refreshments	Pubs at Ludham and Ludham Bridge
Ordnance Survey maps	Landranger 134 (Norwich & The Broads), Explorer OL40 (The Broads)

Looking at the map the River Ant seems to live up to its name – it is a narrow, tortuous waterway connecting Barton Broad with the main network of rivers. The head of navigation is at a tiny village a little way upstream from the Broad though only a few cruisers venture that far. Yet although the Ant may be lacking in stature, its course provides some of the finest scenery of the Broads, at its height in the reaches on each side of How Hill. The walk takes in a delightful village before reaching the riverbank via country lanes and field paths. The How Hill estate now serves as an environmental centre with nature trails and an electric boat providing wildlife water trails (tel. Toad Hole Cottage 01692 678763).

Return to the lane from the Toad Hole Cottage car park and turn left, passing the entrance to How Hill Study Centre. The house was built in 1903 by a Norwich architect as a country retreat though it ended up a grander residence than was originally planned, with elaborate thatched roof inset with dormer windows. Certainly no other house on the Broads can rival its commanding position or landscaped grounds. It stands on one of the rare Broadland hills which just tops 98ft (30m). This is appreciated as the lane drops down after the house through an avenue of fine oak trees. Turn right **A** just before a house as the lane levels on to a pleasant grassy bridleway shaded by more oaks, newly planted ones filling gaps on the left.

The bridleway swings left – follow it for a few paces but look for a path on the right **B**, by an oak tree, which strikes across the field towards a gap in the hedge on the other side, thus cutting off a corner. The path crosses the next field heading directly towards the tower of Ludham church and joins a field-edge track. Turn right on to this to reach a lane and keep ahead on this. Turn left at a T-junction and then keep ahead at a staggered crossroads to walk past modern housing and the village school to reach Ludham village centre. Turn right after the school. The King's Arms is opposite the church. Keep ahead to pass the east end of the church and pleasing 18th-century houses, one of them thatched.

The lane is quiet and pleasant but

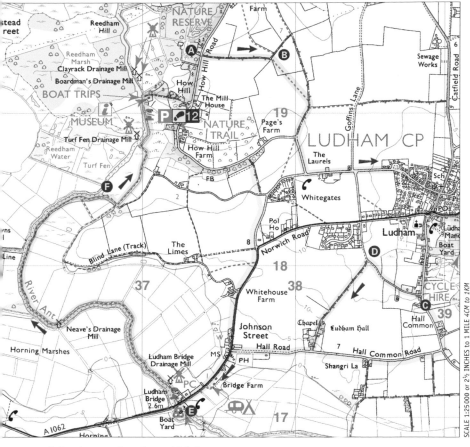

watch for the next junction, which is well concealed. This is Lovers' Lane, a turn on the right **C** just before a thatched cottage. Walk down this narrow lane, which soon becomes a grassy track running down the edge of a field. At this point it may seem that you are walking back to Ludham, but at the far side of the field the track is joined by another from the southwest. Turn sharply left on to this **D** to head towards buildings on the skyline. To the right of the track is Ludham Hall. The chapel shown on the map is now used as a farm shed, with bricked-up windows and an entrance knocked in its east end, wide enough to accommodate tractors. The rest of the hall retains its ancient beauty. To the left of the farmyard is a fine early-18th-century barn, which

unfortunately wears a modern roof. Walk through the farmyard and turn right on to the lane, which leads to the main road. Turn left at this junction to reach the Dog Inn within a few yards.

Continue along the main road after the pub – there is a good pavement on the right of the carriageway. Pass the toilets and telephone box and then turn right **E** to leave the road before the bridge to walk on the riverbank. The reed-fringed path follows the river as it makes a great meander westwards to the foot of Browns Hill. How Hill can now be seen in the distance to the right with a well-preserved drainage mill in the foreground.

The path leaves the riverbank at a dyke **F** and heads toward a wood. When it gets close to this the path divides – take the left fork. Tall reeds screen the vista at first but there are soon views of the How Hill estate with its small lake. Soon afterwards the path is back on the riverbank, which is always busy during holiday months. Walk past the frontage of How Hill and, just before a thatched boathouse, turn right away from the river and cross a footbridge to walk past Toad Hole Cottage, once a marshman's home but now a Broads Authority information centre and free museum with artefacts showing how such people lived in the 19th and early 20th centuries. The garden is planted with herbs that were essential for cooking and medicines at this time. From the cottage, walk to the right of the big house across the greensward to return to the car park at the starting point. ●

Drainage mill on the River Ant at How Hill

Mannington Hall, Wolterton and the Bure valley

Start	Mannington Hall car park
Distance	6½ miles (10.5km)
Approximate time	2½ hours
Parking	Car park open daily from 09.00 until dusk
Refreshments	Pubs at Wolterton and Itteringham, tearoom at Mannington Hall in season
Ordnance Survey maps	Landranger 133 (North East Norfolk), Explorer 252 (Norfolk Coast East)

Both Mannington Hall and Wolterton Park, the family homes of Lord and Lady Walpole, have trails within the grounds that give the visitor opportunities to view the outside of the houses from the surrounding gardens and park. This walk allows glimpses of both houses: Wolterton grand in the classical manner and Mannington smaller and more intimate, girdled with a moat. After Wolterton the return leg of the route uses charming byways and field paths to return to Mannington.

Walk past the information centre in the car park (where you pay for a ticket if the kiosk is open, alternatively there is an honesty box) following the 'Boardwalk' waymark. There is a length of beautiful grassy track passing venerable oak trees before the famous boardwalk. This takes you across a wide area of wetland where there are information boards giving details of the flora and fauna. When the path divides, it does not matter which way you go as both paths lead to the Scrape, a large pool that has been made for waterfowl with a hide overlooking it. Having investigated this, continue for a few yards to a junction with a public footpath **A** and turn right on to another green way lined with oak trees. At the end of the track go over a stile into a meadow. Keep Hall Farm to the

left and at the end of the meadow, turn left to go through a gate by the corner of the farmyard. Bear right along the farm drive to reach the road. Cross this to a lane going to Wolterton and Wickmere.

At the next junction, turn left and then after ½ mile (800m) turn right into the aptly named Wall Road. If you are tall enough you will be able to see Wolterton Hall and the romantic ruins of the medieval church, abandoned in 1737 when the hall was almost complete. Horatio Walpole, brother of Sir Robert, engaged Thomas Ripley to build the house. Ripley was the architect of the Admiralty in London and had also worked at Houghton Hall, but it was Wolterton that confirmed his reputation. In the early 19th century the house was enlarged by George Stanley Repton.

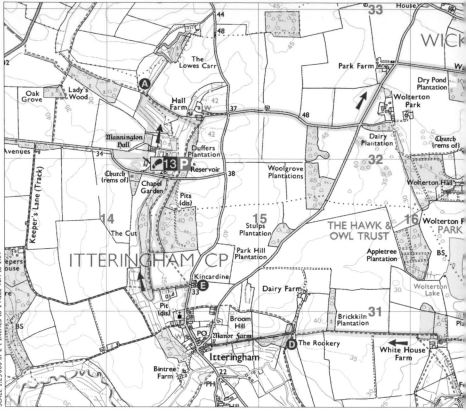

0	200	400	600	800 METRES	1	
						KILOMETRES
						MILES
0	200	400	600 YARDS	½		

Continue along the road after the main drive into the park to come to the Saracen's Head and take the track opposite **B** which leads southwards past an oak tree marked on the map, important because it signified a parish boundary. This is a lovely part of the walk: open countryside at first and then woodland. Turn right when the track meets a lane.

After a patch of woodland on the right, the surfaced road ends when it swings to the right **C** towards White House Farm. If you have time, detour to the left down the footpath to the river, which is at its best here. Continue to White House Farm and keep ahead between the farmhouse and a cottage. You may be tempted by the footpath leading to the left here down to river-side meadows, but be warned that in summer you may find a bull in a meadow and a bridge is lacking to take the path over a ditch, so walkers may well find themselves with boots full of mire. Thus it is recommended that you continue along the field-edge track after White House Farm, which climbs steadily while heading due west.

Keep ahead with the hedge to the right when the track swings away to the left. After a little way the path moves to the other side of the hedge and eventually drops to a stile and a broad track **D**. Cross this to a gate opposite and follow the shady lane on the other side, which seems once to have been surfaced. After another gate the right of way runs through a lovely meadow before coming to Itteringham Manor Farm, 'an unusually perfect example of the late seventeenth-century house', according to Pevsner, dating from 1707. The track

Walk past the church (note the antique AA sign on the end of a cottage nearly opposite – it is 121¼ miles to London from here! Walk that ¼ mile (400m) and then take the footpath on the left **E** which follows the right side of a hedge. The path goes into the wood at the bottom of the field, crosses a plank bridge, and turns right. After passing through a tunnel of rhododendrons, the path joins the stream – the vegetation has the character of jungle here. Climb a stile to emerge into full daylight and a narrow meadow.

The right of way follows the right-hand side of the meadow to the lane, which passes Mannington Hall. Turn left and look up the main drive for a good view of the hall from the south. It dates from 1460 though it was greatly altered by the 4th Earl of Orford in 1864. His tomb is in the ruined church, which is to the left of the lane and is reached via Chapel Walk if you have bought a ticket for the gardens. Its inscription implies that his lordship did not trust his family to provide a monument so he had this one put up himself.

Turn right when the lane swings left to return to the car park at the starting point. ●

past the house comes out in the middle of the village. Turn left and then right, taking the road to Mannington (the pub lies to the left, on the other side of the bridge).

Moated Mannington Hall

The Great Ouse from Downham Market

Start	Downham Market
Distance	6½ miles (10.5km)
Approximate time	3 hours
Parking	Pay and Display car park next to council offices
Refreshments	Pubs at Stowbridge (closed during the day on Mondays and Tuesdays) and Wimbotsham
Ordnance Survey maps	Landranger 143 (Ely & Wisbech), Explorer 236 (King's Lynn, Downham Market & Swaffham)

The 'Adventurers' who drained the Fens in the 17th century evoke admiration for their courage and engineering skill. Their legacy has been inherited by modern river authorities who continue the fight to keep the North Sea from invading. The walk takes you along the east bank of the Great Ouse with the modern Relief Channel running alongside. After leaving the riverbank the walk uses footpaths and country roads to return.

Downham Market is a bustling little town situated on the edge of the Fens whose fame rests on the fact that Nelson spent some of his schooldays here. Its streets have their share of picturesque town houses and cottages, and there is a large parish church.

🥾 Leave the car park and turn right to pass the Health Centre and Methodist church. Keep ahead into a cul-de-sac where the road swings right and turn left down Paradise Lane and then left at the main road. This part of the town has buildings built of dark brown carrstone, apart from flint, the county's only building stone. Cross the railway to come to Hythe Bridge, which spans the Relief Channel (the Hythe is the narrow strip of land between the two waterways). Denver Sluice can be seen in the distance upriver. Go over the stile **Ⓐ** to the western bank of the Relief Channel,

which gives a good view of the town as you walk northwards. To the left the horizon seems limitless over the vastness of the Fens.

Cross the narrow strip of meadow and climb up to the bank of the River Ouse where there is a sandy track (note that at the parish boundary the footpath becomes a bridleway, for no obvious reason). This is a part of the Fens' Rivers Way, an excellent 3-mile (4.8km) stretch

Sunset over the Great Ouse at Stowbridge

where you can appreciate the unique character of the Fens. Home Farm, on the west bank of the river, is just 3ft (0.9m) above mean sea level!

Stowbridge can be seen in the distance from the start of the riverbank section on a clear day. The pub by the bridge has long been closed but by turning right away from the river bridge **B** you come to The Heron, a fisherman's pub where the talk is often about the giant zander that may be caught here.

Cross the bridge over the Relief Channel and turn back along the east bank towards Downham. After $^1/_2$ mile (800m) look for a railway cottage which was obviously once occupied by a crossing-keeper. Go through the gates here to cross the railway **C** and walk through a scrapyard to a track leading towards Gullpit Farm. Just before reaching it, leave the track by turning right **D** on to a path along the edge of a wood. When it reaches a road, turn right and follow this to the road junction at the centre of Wimbotsham.

Turn right here before the pub and the school to take the main road towards Downham. Just before Lower Farm leave the road to the right **E**, taking a footpath heading towards a wood. This is a pleasant grassy track with a wide view to the left. Bear left when the track divides to walk down the side of Kingston's Plantation with Downham church tower ahead. The

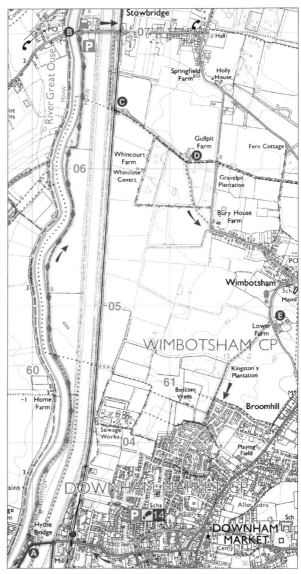

SCALE 1:27 777 or about 2¼ INCHES to 1 MILE 3.6CM to 1KM

right of way crosses a footbridge and passes behind new housing before turning left to reach a road. Go right on to this (Wimbotsham Road), keep ahead when it swings right, and then turn left into Batchcroft Close. At the top of this, turn right on to a footpath that leads back to the start at the council offices (on the left when the footpath reaches the road). ●

Hardley Cross from Chedgrave

Start	Chedgrave
Distance	6½ miles (10.5km)
Approximate time	3½ hours
Parking	Church car park on weekdays. On-street parking in Chedgrave. Public car parks in Loddon
Refreshments	Pubs and cafés at Chedgrave and Loddon
Ordnance Survey maps	Landranger 134 (Norwich & The Broads), Explorer OL40 (The Broads)

The Broads Authority cuts back nettles and grass in early summer so it may be best to avoid this walk in May or early June. Certainly do not try it in shorts before the cut. The outward stretch of the walk is on a quiet road and it takes little more than 30 minutes to reach Hardley Dike. From this point the walking is on riverbank, the highlight being walking the narrow causeway between the River Chet and Hardley Flood – a secret beauty spot.

Leave the car park by turning right down Hardley Road. This quiet highway is soon out into the country and the view to the right is pleasing, the skyline being richly wooded. After Dairy Farm the sugar beet factory at Cantley is an obvious feature of the landscape. Keep ahead at the only junction towards Hardley Staithe to climb the flank of Broom Hill, at 56ft (17m) a formidable summit in this district where some fields are below sea level.

About half an hour of brisk walking will take you to lovely Hardley church with the staithe **A** a little further on. Walk down the right-hand side of the dyke to pass a notice that tells how a staithe may well have been here since Saxon times. The present straight dyke was dug in the 19th century to replace the old one, which was tortuous. The pub that once stood at the head of

the staithe disappeared long ago.

The bank of the River Yare is soon reached and you are able to turn your back on the beet factory for a short while. A wide meander brings it back into view, but there are plenty of other distractions, with reed warblers to be

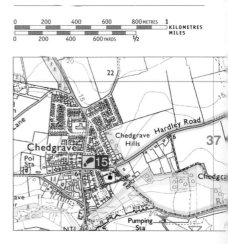

seen in the rushes and grebes playing 'last across' with the river traffic. If the riverbank has not yet been cut you will find the thistles unmerciful.

Hardley Cross **B** marks the end of the jurisdiction of Norwich on the course of the Yare below the city. A signboard on the opposite bank of the River Chet, which joins with the Yare here, says that it is 3½ miles (5.6km) to Loddon – it is a mile (1.6km) less as the crow flies. Hardley Flood is one of Broadland's best-kept secrets – a mile-long (1.6km) stretch of open water with a wood at its eastern end and meadows on its northern shore. It plays host to a wonderful variety of waterfowl, while giant pike lurk beneath its surface. The path runs along a narrow causeway

Hardley Cross

with the river close on the left. Continue to walk along the riverbank at Chedgrave Common to reach the point just before the boatyards, where the right of way swings away from the river to the drive serving the boatyards. This drive takes you back to Hardley Road and Chedgrave church at the starting point. ●

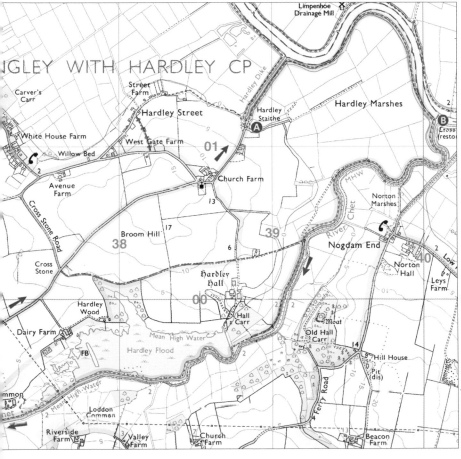

Boudicca's Way – Shotesham and Saxlingham Nethergate

Start	Shotesham church
Distance	7 miles (11.3km)
Approximate time	3½ hours
Parking	Church car park at Shotesham (not on Sundays or festivals)
Refreshments	Pub at Shotesham
Ordnance Survey maps	Landranger 134 (Norwich & The Broads), Explorer 237 (Norwich)

Boudicca's Way is a long distance footpath that winds its way through the choicest scenery in south Norfolk, principally running north to south from Norwich to the county boundary. This route follows sections of the one dedicated to Boudicca, but also uses less popular but equally well-maintained footpaths across some of the loveliest Norfolk countryside to be found south of Norwich. The romantic ruins of St Mary's Church, hidden in a wood at Saxlingham, are a highlight of the walk.

Shotesham is one of East Anglia's most attractive villages, with red-roofed cottages spaced amongst rich meadows.

From the church car park walk to the war memorial and then take the footpath dropping down to a track which begins by the bridge. This is part of Boudicca's Way, a gravel drive initially and then a well-used woodland path with a stream to the right. After crossing the stream the path climbs out of the wood and the tower of Shotesham's other church can be seen to the right with the ruined tower of St Martin's close by. The path crosses a field and then follows the edge of another one with the hedge to the left.

Turn left at the end of the field **Ⓐ** to continue on Boudicca's Way, a field track on the edge of trees. There is a wonderful view when the Way (now a path) cuts across the neck of two fields to the corner of Great Wood. A little further on there is a bench overlooking a patch of ground near Stubb's Green, which becomes a mauve sea of lady's-smock (cuckoo-flower) in early spring.

Just beyond there is a complicated meeting of paths at the corner of the wood **Ⓑ** – go right here to follow the edge of the wood on a grassy path and climb gently southwards. After crossing a plank bridge the path comes to the end of the wood. Keep ahead across the field to reach Wash Lane **Ⓒ** and turn right. Within a few steps you see a waymark for the Saxlingham Nethergate village walk. Turn left on to this

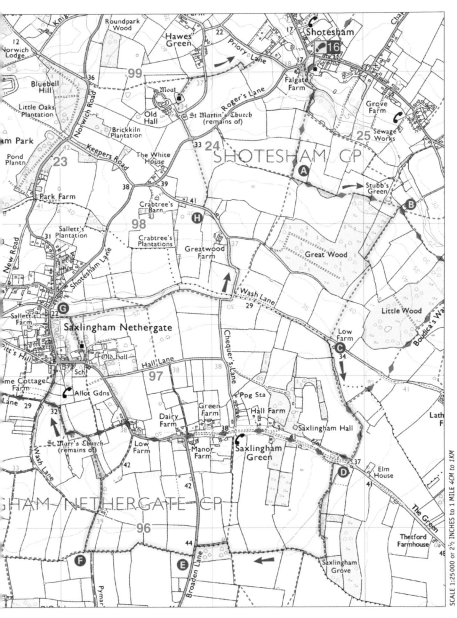

SCALE 1:25000 or 2½ INCHES to 1 MILE 4CM to 1KM

footpath and pass behind an old barn on the edge of the field, crossing another plank bridge. Keep ahead on the right bank of the ditch after Boudicca's Way rejoins from the left, bearing right at the end of a field to skirt a pond and come to Saxlingham Green. Cross the road here to the footpath opposite **D**, in fact a farm track leading towards a belt of trees.

The path skirts Saxlingham Grove and at the end of the wood keep ahead when a path leaves to the left over a plank bridge – the landscape is now high and flat, but there may well be skylarks overhead and cowslips lining the ditches. Turn right at the end of the

Daffodils at Sho.tesham

field and then left to reach the road walking past a new spinney on the left. Turn left, walk for 50 yds (46m), and then leave it to the right **E**, crossing a plank bridge to join a field-edge path. Pass the concealed junction with Pymar's Lane on the left, turn right at the corner of the field **F** and walk down to a spinney of conifers. Keep ahead, crossing a steep-sided ditch to a path on the left side of the spinney, and ignoring a path that goes to the right. The route rejoins Boudicca's Way again at a crossways – keep ahead on to a sunken bridleway, which rises to show the remains of St Mary's Church through the foliage to the left. Turn right after the church to head towards the village. A sunken track leads to another crossways. Turn right here and then at the road turn right again.

At the beautiful Old Hall, turn right into the churchyard and pass the church to find a gate on the north side of the churchyard. Follow the path for 100 yds (91m) after this before turning right over a stile **G** to reach a watery path leading through a narrow meadow. After this it crosses a vast field to reach a hedgerow, which it follows with the hedge on the left to Chequer's Lane. Keep ahead to cross a ford and walk along the lane past Greatwood farmyard and a modern bungalow with a paddock. After the latter leave the lane to the right over a plank bridge **H** and on to a field-edge path. Where electric lines cross, turn left to traverse a field towards a church. At the road continue heading for the two church towers. Walk through the churchyard of St Mary's to a footpath at the northeast corner. Shotesham village, overlooked by its lovely church, is now seen to the right. Bear right, with the ditch to the right, to come to a lane, and cross it to walk on to Priory Lane, where you turn right back to the starting point. ●

Langmere and Devil's Punchbowl

Start	Norfolk Wildlife Trust Reserve, East Wretham, 3 miles (4.8km) north-east of Thetford on west side of A1075
Distance	6 miles (9.7km). Shorter version 5½ miles (8.9km)
Approximate time	3½ hours (2½ hours for shorter version)
Parking	At start
Refreshments	None en route
Ordnance Survey maps	Landranger 144 (Thetford & Diss), Explorer 229 (Thetford Forest in The Brecks)

Norfolk's Breckland provides some wonderful heathland and forest walking, and while the grid-like layout of the forest rides should make navigation easy, in practice it is easy to become confused. It may seem ridiculous, but it is advisable to use a compass hereabouts, especially as dusk falls early in the forest. This is the reason for the alternative route – a long stretch of rough gravel track instead of a series of more obscure grassy ones. Of course, a third alternative is to return from the Punchbowl the way you went on the Drove Road, which is hardly less pleasing. Note that dogs are not allowed in the nature reserve and that the way through the forest may be restricted during army manoeuvres or in the shooting season.

The Norfolk Wildlife Trust Reserve at East Wretham Heath was the first reserve to be established in Breckland when it was acquired in 1938.

Much of the county's 'Breck' (land which was once cultivated but abandoned when its sandy soil became impoverished) is covered by forest, while the largest area of heath is used by the army as a battle training area. Thus fragments showing the original landscape are rare, the East Wretham Heath being one of the best of them with its two meres surrounded by woodland and sandy grassland grazed only by sheep and rabbits.

From the car park at the Warden's House go through the kissing-gate on to a grassy track heading towards a fine group of Scots' pines. The path is waymarked green and white up to the next kissing-gate, where the two routes divide, the green path going right to take a delightful circuitous route through the wood while the white route takes a more direct route to the exit from the reserve, closer to Langmere. A birdwatchers' hide allows visitors to view wildfowl on the water. Its level fluctuates from year to year, season to season, and occasionally the mere dries up altogether, usually in winter after summer drought. Curlew and snipe are sometimes to be seen feeding on exposed mud while widgeon and shelduck are also winter visitors.

The two routes join near the western exit from the reserve **A** which is over a stile on to a track known locally as the Drove. This is part of a long distance footpath from Ely to Bury St Edmunds called the Hereward Way, which is probably prehistoric. Certainly one could imagine a group of Saxon rebels making their way along this ancient road.

Turn right to head westwards but be aware that cyclists enjoy using it as well and can approach swiftly and silently from the rear. After about a mile (1.6m) the waymarked route swings left and becomes narrow for a short distance

before reaching a road **B**. Cross this to another road opposite – note the unnamed mere to the right which is within the Battle Area. Where the road bends **C** there is access to a picnic site. Walk down to see the Devil's Punch-bowl on the left, a sinister-looking dark puddle of water at the bottom of steep, wooded slopes.

Those with concerns about forest navigation may prefer an alternative route back to the start. They can walk back to **B** *by turning right along the road for about 200 yds (183m) and then taking the gravel track on the left that runs parallel to the Drove. After two miles, at the end of an area of cleared forest on the right, the track swings to the right and there is a forestry sign to the right with 67/67 on it. Turn left here on to a grassy track, which soon takes you back to the Drove opposite the*

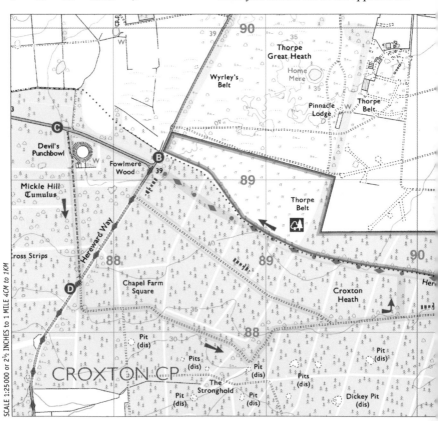

SCALE 1:25000 or 2½ INCHES to 1 MILE 4CM to 1KM

stile out of the nature reserve **A**. *Note that if you walk beyond the 67/67 junction you will soon come to electric lines and realise that you have missed an important turn.*

If you have more confidence – and preferably a compass – you will enjoy tackling the slightly longer route that uses lesser-used paths. Keep ahead from the Punch-bowl, passing a house on the left and passing through a barrier where there is a footpath sign. The lovely grassy track heads directly southwards and soon comes to a road **D**. Cross the road and go past another barrier on to a track that swings left around a deep pit not dissimilar to the Punchbowl (though this one may be a bomb crater, considering by the age of the trees). Keep ahead at a crossways where a forestry sign bears the figures 6 and 62

The Devil's Punchbowl

(the main track goes to the right). Leave the major track at the next crossways too, keeping ahead on a narrow grassy path heading south-east and with young trees to the left.

Keep ahead once more, leaving the main path to go left, even though the path ahead seems to vanish into tall grass and bracken. This swings left (to the north), crosses a broad sandy track, and then joins the Drove. Turn right to reach **A** and continue on the Drove to enjoy an excellent view of Langmere and the smaller Ringmere.

There is a memorial stone to Sydney Herbert Long who founded the Norfolk Naturalists' Trust in 1929 (now renamed the Norfolk Wildlife Trust) and died ten years later.

Just before the track meets the A1075 a stile gives access to a path leading directly across the heath to the starting point at the Warden's House. ●

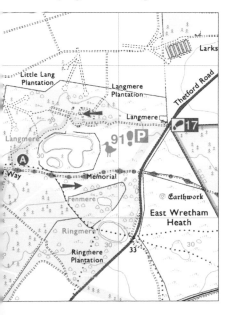

Peddars Way, Fring and Sedgeford

Start	Fring church
Distance	7 miles (11.3km)
Approximate time	2½ hours
Parking	On quiet lane near church
Refreshments	Pub at Sedgeford
Ordnance Survey maps	Landranger 132 (North West Norfolk), Explorer 250 (Norfolk Coast West)

This walk goes a little way to dispel the myth of Norfolk's flatness, and there are two stretches of the Peddars Way here that may make you pause to catch breath. The views from these heights are splendid, and the country byways used are rarely disturbed by traffic.

The quiet lane that runs past Fring church heads northwest and drops down past a wood before coming to a small bridge.

Turn right **A** on to a narrow footpath, which leads to a broad grassy track between fields. The track makes lovely walking, typical of the Peddars Way, the long distance route that runs from the west Norfolk coast at Holme next the Sea to the border with Suffolk on Breckland's Knettishall Heath, a distance of 46 miles (74km). Its name is probably medieval and may derive from 'peds', the semicircular wicker panniers that were used to carry goods to market. However, the road itself dates from the early years of the Roman occupation and may have connected Colchester and York via a ferry that crossed the Wash from Holme. It also links Norfolk with the Icknield Way, a prehistoric track that ran along the crest of chalky upland to end near Avebury in Wiltshire.

The track climbs to the top of Dove Hill, its summit nearly 150ft (46m) above sea level, almost an Everest in Norfolk. After the wood here the track crosses to the other side of the hedgerow, and Magazine Cottage at Sedgeford can be seen ahead. This delightful little building on the edge of the village looks like a chapel but was built during the Civil War to serve as a Royalist arms' store. The le Strange family at Old Hunstanton owned property at Sedgeford and were supporters of the King, so that it is probable that they had the Magazine built in a style that gave no hint of its purpose.

The track becomes a path which swings left and then right to pass the cluster of cottages known as Littleport and then reach the road on the outskirts of Sedgeford **B**. Turn right here if you wish to see Magazine Cottage, otherwise turn left to walk into the village on the roadside footpath. Take

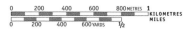

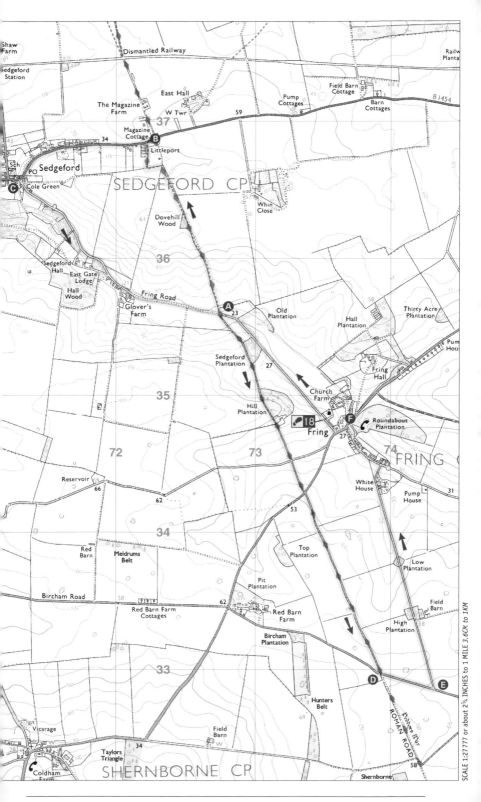

SCALE 1:27777 or about 2¼ INCHES to 1 MILE 3.6CM to 1KM

the turn to the left **C** to Fring to continue on the route unless you prefer to visit the King William IV pub, which is further up the main street on the left.

The leafy lane passes the drive to Sedgeford Hall on the right and a roadside nature reserve before coming to where it crosses the Peddars Way **A**. Turn right here to climb the hill towards woodland. Many cyclists use the track and may approach silently from the rear. After the large house in Hill Plantation the track is surfaced and soon reaches a road. Cross this road and the next one, which is reached within a short distance, to walk along the track,

which dips and rises as it heads southeast. Bircham windmill can be seen in the distance to the left.

Turn left at the next road **D** – the cranes on the horizon are at the Training Centre at Bircham Newton where construction workers are taught to use heavy machinery. Take the turn on the left **E** after nearly $\frac{1}{2}$ mile (800m) on a surfaced bridleway – a quiet byway that takes the walker back to Fring.

Turn left at the road **F** to walk past the ponds and war memorial and then turn right back to the church. ●

Walking the ancient Peddars Way

Denver Sluice – a three rivers walk

Start	Bridge over Cut-Off Channel at Fordham
Distance	7½ miles (12.1km)
Approximate time	3½ hours
Parking	Car park adjacent to bridge
Refreshments	Pubs at Denver and Hilgay (latter also has a riverside tearoom)
Ordnance Survey maps	Landranger 143 (Ely & Wisbech), Explorer 228 (March & Ely)

Walkers are on riverbanks for most of the time on this route, and many will enjoy the stretch along the modest River Wissey to the broad reaches of the River Ouse or the unerring straightness of the Cut-Off Channel. Denver Sluice is the chief component in the elaborate system of Fenland drainage, the focal point of no fewer than seven waterways.

From the car park turn left to cross the bridge over the Cut-Off Channel and turn right on to the bridleway that runs behind the southern bank. On a hot summer's day hundreds of damsel flies sunbathe on the surface of the track. After about ½ mile (800m) the track turns away from the river and passes farm buildings and then divides. Bear left and then right to walk to the left of a spinney and then between hedgeless fields heading towards the trees of Harold Covert. The River Wissey flows at the end of this small wood. Turn right and climb the riverbank **A** to walk towards the railway bridge.

The path goes beneath the bridge to the right over a rickety stile by a concrete post. After another short stretch along the reed-fringed River Wissey the riverbank path brings you to the point where its waters join with those of the Great Ouse **B**.

The walking along the riverbank may be obstructed by thistles and clumps of nettles in places, but sheep graze here and their tracks usually provide a way of avoiding being stung or pricked. Denver's beautiful windmill can be seen to the right, and the 2 miles (3.2km) to the sluice are soon completed. At weekends the river is busy with pleasure boats, amongst them dinghies with colourful sails. Leave the riverbank to climb a stile and join a tree-lined track to reach the bridge over the Relief Channel **C**. Turn left to cross this and so reach the sluice.

Cornelius Vermuyden, a Dutch engineer, was employed by the Duke of Bedford in 1642 to draw up plans for the drainage of the fens, and his scheme still operates today, albeit with sophisticated modern machinery. In addition the Cut-Off Channel (what a boring name for a waterway more than

15 miles (24km) long!) gathers the waters of the rivers Lark, Wissey and Little Ouse and takes them directly to Denver, allowing floodwater to escape more efficiently, without jeopardising the natural beauty of the original waterways. An ambitious scheme to make the Cut-Off Channel navigable for pleasure boats is currently being completed.

The first sluice was constructed in 1834 by John Rennie and this lasted until 1923. The steady shrinkage of the peat as it dried out after drainage (and then was blown away by the wind), plus

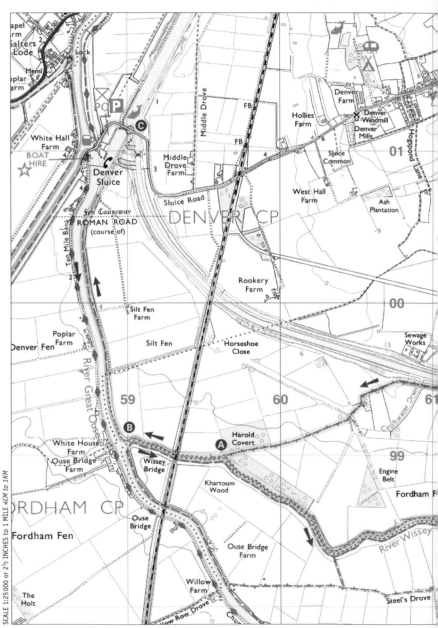

the problems generated by global warming, mean that the Environment Agency has an unenviable responsibility to save the fens from being flooded. The present sluice dates from 1983 and has a massive steel floodgate that can be used to control tidal surges as well as

At Denver Sluice

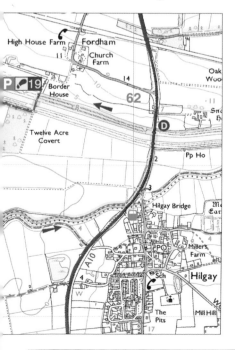

floodwater flowing in the opposite direction, towards the sea.

Cross the sluice if you wish for refreshment at the Jenkyns Arms, an ancient pub popular with fishermen. Otherwise return to the bridge over the Relief Channel **C** and walk along the riverside by the Great Ouse and then the Wissey to reach **B**. Continue along the bank of the Wissey to Hilgay. This is a delightful part of the route, walking by a river that makes leisurely meanders throughout its course and nevertheless is navigated by quite large cruisers. Hilgay eventually comes into view, perched on its 'hill', which achieves a dizzy height of just over 50ft (17m).

The Cross Keys is the nearest pub when you reach the village. Cross the main road and the original bridge to reach it. Otherwise continue walking northwards along the main road, go over the modern road bridge, and then turn left on to the path **D**, heading back to the starting point by the side of the Cut-Off Channel. ●

The Little Ouse from Thetford

Start	Town Bridge, Thetford (or Two Mile Bottom Picnic Place on A134, ½ mile (800m) north-west of factory)
Distance	7½ miles (12.1km) or 5 miles (8km) for shorter route from Two Mile Bottom
Approximate time	2½ hours (1½ hours for shorter route)
Parking	Town Bridge car park, Thetford
Refreshments	Pubs and cafés at Thetford
Ordnance Survey maps	Landranger 144 (Thetford & Diss), Explorer 229 (Thetford Forest in The Brecks)

The route gives easy walking on the old towpath along the bank of the Little Ouse and on grassy or sandy tracks through Thetford Forest. The beauty of the river rivals that of many of the famous Broadland waterways though only canoes are likely to be seen today. Thetford has many fine buildings reflecting its long history and there is an excellent small museum telling its story.

The main town car park has its entrance next to the Anchor Hotel. Cross the road here with the colourful cast-iron Town Bridge to the right. This bridge replaced the wooden St Christopher's Bridge in 1829. Join the riverside footpath. This used to be known as the Haling (probably Norfolk dialect for 'hauling') Path in the days when fen lighters were drawn upstream to Thetford from King's Lynn, bringing coal to the town and returning with wool and grain. In the heyday of steam Thetford was famous for its fairground and agricultural machinery made by Messrs Burrell.

This is the start of the Little Ouse Path, which runs from here to Brandon. It goes beneath the town's original bypass, which proved inadequate for modern traffic almost as soon as it was opened in 1968. Before this all traffic had to pass over Town Bridge. The remains of Thetford Priory are on the opposite side of the river but will not be seen, at any rate in summer.

🖉 Cross the river by the footbridge to continue on the northern bank and go beneath another road bridge and then the modern bypass. After this there is a lovely lake to the right and the path becomes grassy. Abbey Heath Weir Ⓐ makes a lovely spot for a picnic, with grassy banks sloping down to the river.

Keep on the riverside path, which goes as far as the bend in the river where it swings right and then left to enter woodland. The path is sometimes illegally used by cyclists who may approach silently from behind you. Nevertheless, walking is pleasant, with the river to the left and deciduous trees

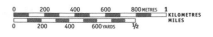

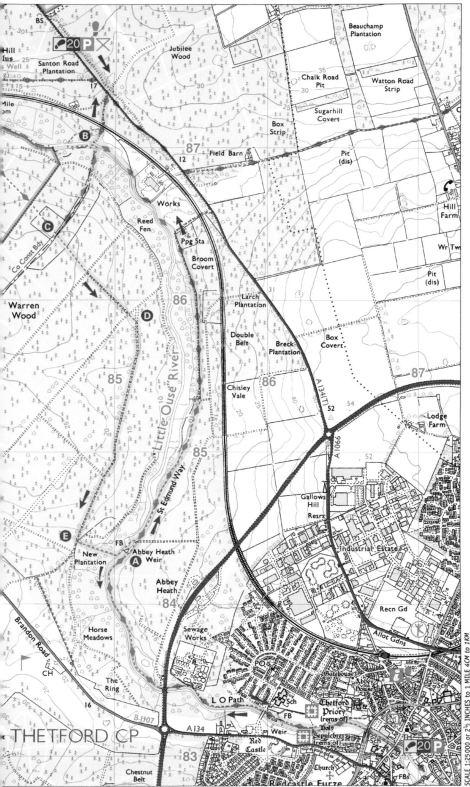

THE LITTLE OUSE FROM THETFORD ● **63**

Thetford

giving shade or shelter.

A tall white chimney appears ahead belonging to a factory making building materials. The right of way follows the left side of an area of rough ground used by moto-cross bikes to a permissive path that runs between the factory fence and the river. Keep ahead by the river after this and pass to the left of a Guide and Scout Centre to reach a footbridge **B**.

The shorter route starts from Two Mile Bottom picnic place. Walk down the road to the driveway to Bidwell Guide and Scout Centre and pass beneath the railway. Fork left after this (a notice here warns of low-flying model aircraft) to reach the riverside. Turn right to **B**.

On the other side of the river cross a low piece of ground and then climb a bank to be faced with a broad firebreak. Keep ahead on this to follow a footpath sign to Brandon. At the top of the firebreak **C**, turn left on to a track bearing waymarks showing (seemingly) hooves and cartwheels. Ignore similar waymarks at the next firebreak by keeping

ahead on a sandy track heading towards radio masts. Keep ahead again to cross a large area that has recently been re-planted. The track bends southwards **D** so that the radio masts are now to the left and the tall factory chimney directly behind you. This is a pleasant part of the route and you are unlikely to meet other walkers. After crossing another replanted area the track descends to a major junction. Take the narrow path to the left here **E** – the right of way has been marked with yellow paint on the tree trunks but this may well fade.

The shady path descends to a ditch and may be muddy largely due to its use by vandals on motor bikes. The situation may be particularly bad where a wooden footbridge crosses the ditch (hopefully some of the motor bikes lie beneath the mud). Cross Abbey Heath Weir **A** and turn right to retrace your steps to Thetford.

If you started from Two Mile Bottom Picnic Site turn left and follow the outward route to pass the factory on the riverside path. Before the metal gate turn right to reach the railway bridge, road and picnic site. ●

A Round of Aylsham

Start	Aylsham church
Distance	8½ miles (13.7km)
Approximate time	4 hours
Parking	Buttlands car park (largest, 200 yds/183m south of church, signed to left off Norwich Road); off Burgh Road, right off Norwich Road; Market Place
Refreshments	Pubs and cafés at Aylsham, pub at Marsham
Ordnance Survey maps	Landranger 134 (Norwich & The Broads), Explorer 238 (East Dereham & Aylsham)

Aylsham is a beautiful market town, old buildings surrounding a notable church and roads radiating from its centre in all directions. It lies in the valley of Broadland's northern river, the Bure, and the walk takes you round two sides of Aylsham passing through a succession of meadows and twice crossing the Bure before following a tributary, delightfully named the Mermaid. Note that a compass is useful as you navigate the water meadows approaching Marsham.

From the Buttlands car park on Mill Road you have a choice.

Head north towards the church tower or, if you wish to see some of Aylsham's oldest buildings, head first south, away from the church and town centre, turn left out of the car park along Mill Road and take the first left turn at the British Legion pub into Hungate Street, which has many interesting timber-framed, brick and thatched houses. Cross the Market Place and walk on through the churchyard, northwards.

Behind railings left of the south-east door of the church lies the grave of Humphry Repton, the landscape gardener (1752–1818).

Aylsham's large church reflects the medieval prosperity of the town when, unusually, its fortune was based on the production of linen rather than wool. Its market was established in the late 13th century, about the time of the building of the church, though its tower is later.

Go through the lichgate at the north side of the churchyard on to Cromer Road and straight on, downhill. Keep ahead to pass Bure Way but turn right down The Meadows to follow a footpath sign pointing to Millgate. Climb a stile, where the road bends right Ⓐ and cross the small meadow diagonally to a stile close to the railway bridge.

(Alternatively, if the meadow is full of cattle you may prefer to follow the road to the right. It soon becomes a narrow path between high hedges, then turn left on to the road. Pass over the two narrow bridges – watch out for traffic – with a pleasant view of Aylsham Mill to the right; once the head of Broads navigation. Take the first road left, by cottages, up and over a bridge across the disused rail track and then turn right to rejoin the route, left up Banningham Road.)

Turn right along the track of the long-abandoned railway, which once went to North Walsham and is now a section of the Weavers Way. There is a lovely glimpse of the River Bure when the path crosses it. Keep on the Weavers Way after going under the road bridge to the small car park, turning right on the road and then left to walk down peaceful Banningham Road – once the main road out of Aylsham to the north but now a cul-de-sac.

The tower of Banningham church can be seen ahead as the road is followed to the right. Turn right at a crossways and follow a short length of green way to the busy A140. There is another green way (Green Lane) opposite which zig-zags its way around fields and is soon close to the old railway line again. Turn right to cross it, leaving the Weavers Way at this point **B** to continue on Green Lane, a delightful track that leads first to a wood and then to a lane. Turn left on to this and then right along Wood Lane, which eventually takes you to Burgh next Aylsham with its beautiful cottages at the crossroads at the centre of the village. Keep ahead here into Church Lane and go through the west side of the churchyard (the church has an exceptionally large chancel of *c.* 1220) to a footbridge over the River Bure.

Take the path on the right after the bridge **C** to cross another bridge and walk with the dyke on the left at first towards a railway bridge. After 100 yds (91m) cross to the other side of the dyke and go through the arch of the bridge. This takes you beneath the narrow-gauge railway going between Aylsham and Wroxham and the Bure Valley Walk that follows it. This provides a short

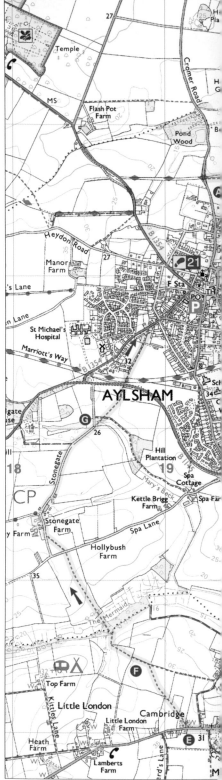

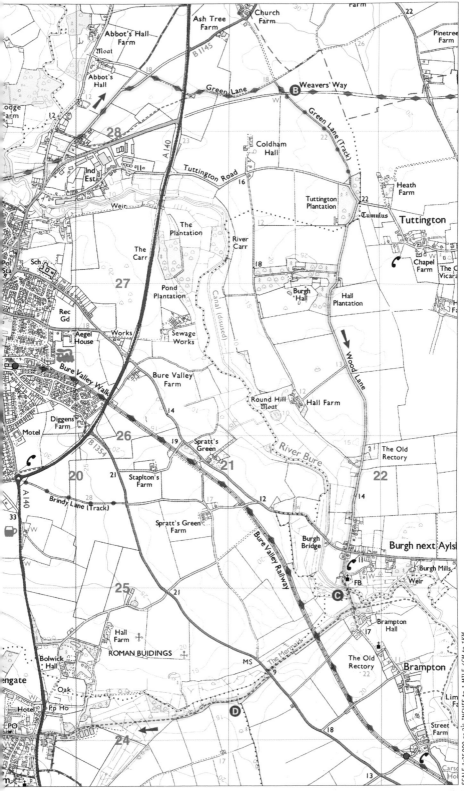

SCALE 1:25000 or 2½ INCHES to 1 MILE 4CM to 1KM

way back to town for those who would like a shorter walk. However, the full circuit still has a lot to offer, notably in the form of the little stream that accompanies the walker now. This has been known as The Mermaid for the last three centuries or so (the reason for the name is a mystery though in medieval times it bore the name 'Hende', an Anglo-Saxon word meaning 'the gracious one'). The more romantic notion of a mermaid swimming up the Bure to find this sparkling stream may be more pleasing. After a stile by a gate the walking is less interesting as the path follows a field edge to the B1354.

Cross the road by turning left to a stile and then walk through a long, narrow meadow grazed by horses. There is a stile in the top right-hand corner of this ⓓ and it may be muddy before and after this. It is tempting to follow the hedge on the left from this point but it is important to note that the right of way heads almost directly westwards from here while the fence bends to the north. Head diagonally across the field towards a large ash tree and a white building that can just be seen beyond it. After a muddy ditch there is a waymark to the left of an electricity pole bearing a transformer. Follow the direction

The church in Burgh next Aylsham

shown by the waymark towards sheds beyond the corner of the boggy field (where one can appreciate how Marsham came to get its name).

A concrete drive leads past the poultry sheds and through a farmyard to the main road. Cross it into the High Street and walk past the post office to climb the hill up to Cranes Lane. Walk along the road for another 100 yds (91m) to find a narrow footpath on the right ⓔ, leading to a stile into a paddock. Follow the direction shown by the waymark to another stile on the far side and then take a diagonal path going through a gap in the hedge to a planting of conifers. Follow frequent waymarks to come to the corner of a large field and cross this diagonally, heading for a cream-coloured house with a red roof.

At the field edge, turn left to the corner of the field ⓕ. The route then strikes across another hedgeless field before it drops down to The Mermaid, which is spanned by a footbridge. On the other side the path goes through a copse and crosses another stream and then climbs to a stile. This gives on to a path across a large field to a lane, and a path on the other side continues by crossing another field towards a farm-house. Turn right along Stonegate, leaving the lane on a sharp left-hand bend ⓖ, where a stile takes a path across a small field with a plank bridge at the centre. Keep walking in the same direction across the next field, making for a short stretch of hedgerow on the far side. Cross the road to steps up the embankment on the other side and cross Marriott's Way to a path running behind bungalows that heads towards Aylsham church. Turn right on to the road, which leads back to the church. The car park is reached by turning right down Mill Road, almost opposite The Feathers public house. ●

Reepham, Marriott's Way and Salle

Start	Reepham church
Distance	9½ miles (15.3km). Shorter version 7 miles (11.3km)
Approximate time	4 hours (2½ hours for shorter version)
Parking	Market Place or car park just to north of it
Refreshments	Pubs in Reepham
Ordnance Survey maps	Landranger 133 (North East Norfolk), Explorer 238 (East Dereham & Aylsham)

Marriott's Way is a national cycleway and footpath that runs from Norwich to Aylsham along the track of the old M&GN railway. It takes its name from William Marriott, its first chief engineer. The outward part of this walk uses the railway but at Themelthorpe a longer alternative is offered which uses green lanes – some of them seldom walked – and footpaths to visit Salle church (pronounced 'Sorl'), one of the finest in Norfolk, before returning to Reepham (pronounced 'Reefham').

It is hardly correct to say start the walk at Reepham church as there are two churches standing in the churchyard with fragments of a third demolished in 1796. St Michael's has a tall tower but is no longer consecrated – it used to serve as the parish church of Whitwell. St Mary's is half hidden by St Michael's and is Reepham's parish church.

🖉 Turn right from the south side of the churchyard and then left after Rookery Farm on to a narrow footpath that runs past modern housing to the right and then a school playing field. Turn right when the path divides **Ⓐ** and right again at a lane, and then go straight over crossroads into Rudd's Lane. Cross a main road to Broomhill Lane and at the end of the school playing field turn left on to a path, following a waymark to Marriott's Way. The pleasantly shady path passes a

massive oak tree on the right and then enters woodland. Take the right fork to climb up the slight embankment and turn right **Ⓑ** on to the former trackbed of the railway which once took passengers from Norwich to Leicester.

One drawback to walking along old railways is that the vegetation on level parts of the track has grown up to screen views of the surrounding countryside. Make the most of the early view to the right over Vale Farm. After this there is a steady uphill gradient and young trees grow on each side. Nevertheless, this is pleasant walking on a good surface, and the road at Themelthorpe is reached about an hour after leaving Reepham. You will probably have read on the noticeboard at the B1145 crossing that the sharp curve that the railway makes here is comparatively modern, dating from 1960, and only lasting until 1985 when concrete manufacture ended at Lenwade.

Alternatively, for the direct way back to Reepham continue to follow the railway line. Leave it where it crosses Kerdiston Lane and follow the latter back to the town centre.

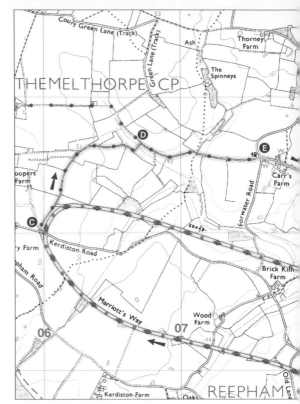

Turn left to pass a crossing-keeper's cottage (aligned for the old railway) and then take a sandy track on the right **C** that climbs to cross a railway bridge. There is also an embankment to the right showing the course of the railway that pre-dated the Themelthorpe curve. After the bridge the green lane is more overgrown but there are views of the countryside. A pair of metal gates enable cattle to cross the track and after this the way becomes even more overgrown. The consoling thought is that at least you are helping to keep this ancient byway clear for walkers in the future though it would help to have secateurs or a billhook.

At a T-junction **D** turn right on to another green way and bear left when it divides. There may be deep ruts hidden

The village sign at Salle

by long grass on this stretch. Keep ahead when you come to a road at a crossways **E** and walk through Kerdiston, comprised of no more than half a dozen cottages and farms. Turn right at a T-junction, pass the white railings of Manor Farm, and turn off the main road to the left and walk past the drive to the farm and a thatched cottage on the right. After this you are on another delightful green way, one which snakes around fields and past cottages and may be muddy in winter. At Kerdy Green a footpath goes off to the right and the track emerges from high hedges and broadens as it passes through a beautiful glade. After this another green way joins from the left. Keep ahead towards Wood Dalling church to the next junction **F** where you turn right down the farm track named Kerdygreen Lane. The tower of Salle church, distinctive with its pinnacles, soon appears ahead.

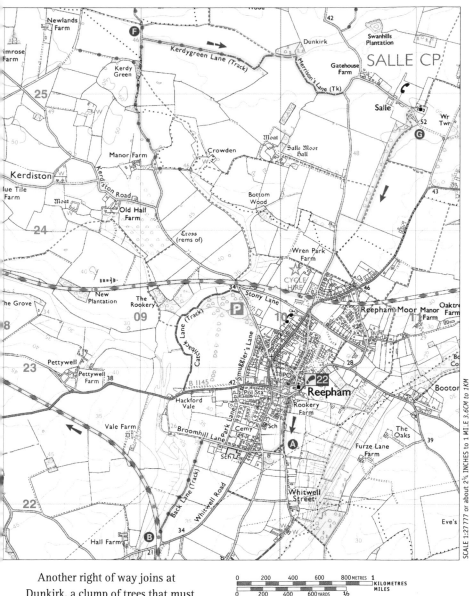

Another right of way joins at Dunkirk, a clump of trees that must have been planted well after the evacuation. Turn left at the lane and then right to reach Salle church, regarded by many as the finest church in Norfolk. It dates from the early 15th century and is a perfect example of the Perpendicular style, the building being completed within about fifty years. It escaped drastic restoration in Victorian times, and many of its medieval furnishings survive. Overall it can hold its own in comparison with any of the more famous East Anglian churches.

From the church cross the cricket field to its far left-hand corner to find a path **G** which goes southwards with a belt of trees to the right. At the end of the trees it turns right to the road. Turn left to return to Reepham, going straight at crossroads to pass the Crown Inn into Ollands Road, which takes you back to the church at the starting point in the centre of the town. ●

Westwick Woods and the Weavers Way

Start	North Walsham station
Distance	8 miles (12.9km)
Approximate time	3 hours
Parking	Weavers Way car park at western end of Station Road
Refreshments	Pubs and restaurants in North Walsham
Ordnance Survey maps	Landranger 133 (North East Norfolk), Explorer 252 (Norfolk Coast East)

The Weavers Way is a 56-mile- (90km) long route running from Cromer to Great Yarmouth. Quite a lot of it follows former railway lines, like the length used here between Felmingham and North Walsham. Much of the outward part of the route runs along the edge of Westwick Woods, beautiful at all times of the year but ablaze with colour in the autumn.

If you come to North Walsham by train you will find Station Road facing you when you leave from the Norwich platform. If you have travelled from the Cromer direction you will have to walk beneath the bridge and then turn right. Station Road heads westwards out of town. After ¹/₂ mile (800m) there is a Weavers Way car park on the left. Car users will start the walk from this point.

Look out for this before Swanton Abbot church

A path leads to the Weavers Way from the car park. Turn left on to a narrow, enclosed path, threatened by brambles and nettles in places. Turn left at the road **Ⓐ**, keeping ahead at the junction to pass Wayside Farm. Just after this, where the road swings right, turn left down Drift Lane **Ⓑ**. This is a pleasant farm track that gives a sight of Felmingham church to the right. Since there are no hedges the views are extensive. Bear left at the corner of the wood and walk for a few yards with the trees to the right. Keep ahead with the hedge to the left when you leave the wood to walk to a pair of isolated oak trees. Turn right here **Ⓒ** to cross the field, following the direction shown on a waymark, to a wooden fence and a stile on the far side.

The stile leads into a wonderful leg of the walk which begins with an avenue of beech and chestnut trees. Although the Perch Lake of the Westwick estate is close to the left, the trees screen a view of it. Likewise it is difficult to see much of Strawberry Hall on the other side. In autumn there are two bonuses to this walk: the splendid colours of the foliage and the abundance of chestnuts and late blackberries.

All too soon the track reaches a gate and then a lane. Turn right **D** and then, at a telephone box, left down a footpath to Swanton Abbott church. Turn right here **E** on to Youngman's Lane and walk past the village school and a

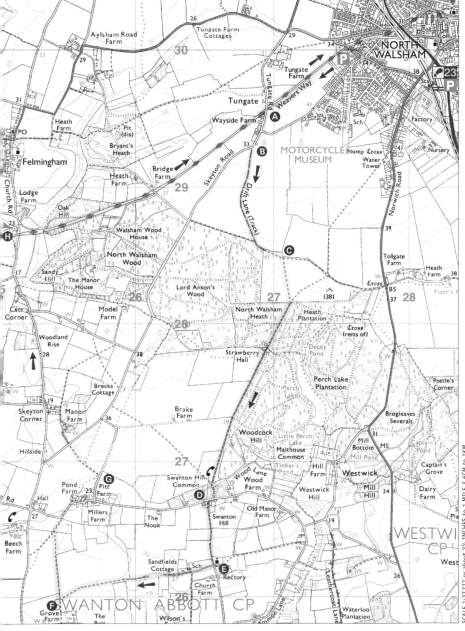

A nesting swan

cottage. After this the way may be nettled for a short way before becoming a distinct field-edge path heading west. Skeyton church is soon seen ahead. After an oak tree which seems to have been struck by lightning the field-edge path ends. Now head across the field ahead, aiming for a gap in the hedge on the far side, with Skeyton church beyond. Go through the gap and turn right **F** on to a little-walked hedgerow path heading north. When the hedgerow ends at a holly tree, keep ahead across a field heading for a post.

At the post veer right towards an electricity post with a waymark just beyond. Here you come to a lane. Turn right, walk past the pond and then turn left on to a lane to North Walsham. Just before the top of the hill look for a waymark in the hedge to the left **G**, pointing across a field towards a clump of trees. When you reach these they prove to be an avenue lining the drive to Manor Farm. Cross the lane and walk

down the drive and through the farmyard, keeping on the concrete track. A short length of road leads past houses to Chapel Lane. Turn right and keep ahead past the Corner House and climb the hill towards Felmingham church in the distance. Further roads go off to right and left, but continue heading for the church and go beneath a railway bridge. Turn left into the car park after this and go through a gate before turning left on to the Weavers Way **H** to pass the platform of the station, used by just four trains a day in each direction at its zenith in 1922. The line is part of the one that used to run from King's Lynn to Great Yarmouth via Melton Constable.

The old railway trackbed gives excellent walking though the trees that have grown up on the lineside and screen the views that passengers might have enjoyed. North Walsham Wood is an extensive planting of young trees, after which the way crosses the road at Tungate **A** and soon reaches the Weavers Way car park on Station Road at the starting point. ●

Weeting Castle from Santon Downham

Start	Santon Downham, 3 miles (4.8km) east of Brandon
Distance	9½ miles (15.3km)
Approximate time	4 hours
Parking	Forest Enterprise car park at Santon Downham
Refreshments	Pubs and cafés in Brandon, pub at Weeting
Ordnance Survey maps	Landranger 144 (Thetford & Diss), Explorer 229 (Thetford Forest in The Brecks)

The opening riverside section between Santon Downham and Thetford is delightful, with views of meadows and woods on the opposite bank which lie in Suffolk. At times the vegetation, including nettles, can be head high so that it is inadvisable to wear shorts. After touching Brandon, the way turns northwards to Weeting, with its lovely church and ruined castle. After this the route follows forest tracks near the famous flint mines of Grime's Graves (a visit there will add 2 miles (3.2km) or so to the total) before descending gently back to the Little Ouse.

Walk to the bridge over the Little Ouse from the car park, cross the river and then turn left **A**, descending steps to reach the path on its northern bank. The path runs by a ditch at first, with the railway line beyond. The lovely landscapes to be seen on the other side of the river, made up of meadows, trees and cattle, could be the subjects of paintings by Constable or Cotman. Keep a wary eye on the path as snakes enjoy sunbathing on sandy patches.

As you progress westwards the vegetation grows higher in summer, even though the authorities do their best to keep the path clear. One of the features of this walk is the number of butterflies likely to be encountered in high summer, together with less welcome insects. The path follows every twist and turn of the river, and it will

take at least an hour before the first of two footbridges is reached. After the second the going improves as the path passes the head of navigation and the small staithe. Follow the bridleway signs to the main road and turn right to pass the Ram and Brandon House hotels.

After crossing the railway, fork left on to the Weeting road and then immediately turn left again **B** down Fengate Drove, an appropriate name, as once the industrial units are passed, it becomes apparent that the fenland lies to the left of the sandy track. Ragwort abounds in the fields in the summer. Steam engines are kept in a paddock opposite Fengate Farm, a reminder that Weeting hosts a famous annual steam rally. Keep ahead at the road and again ahead when, after about 200 yds (183m), it bends to the right. Pass Jubilee Close

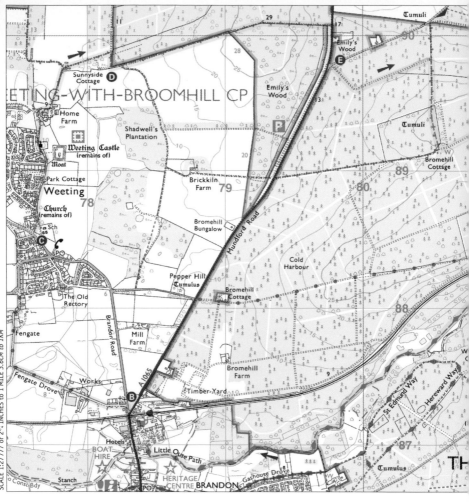

SCALE 1:27777 or 2¼ INCHES to 1 MILE 3.6CM to 1KM

0	200	400	600	800 METRES	1
					KILOMETRES
					MILES
0	200	400	600 YARDS	½	

and then turn right in front of a row of thatched cottages to come to the Weeting village sign and main road **C**. Turn left here if you wish to visit The Saxon inn, otherwise continue on the route by crossing the main road to follow the sign towards Weeting Castle.

Bungalows are to the left and open fields to the right as you walk along the eastern edge of the village to the castle and church. The former was built c. 1130 by Hugh de Plais, the tenant of the Earl of Surrey. The lovely round-towered church is said to date from the 12th century but was practically rebuilt

in 1868. Weeting Hall, a 'large and handsome mansion', was demolished in 1952.

Walk past the church and go through the yard of Home Farm, turning right and then left to skirt outbuildings. The sandy track leads round the back of Sunnyside Cottage. Turn right at the T-junction and then bear left at the next junction **D**, leaving the village circular walk for a green track that runs by the edge of the forest. The trees to the right belong to Shadwell's Plantation, commemorating Thomas Shadwell, the poet, who died in 1691 and was born in Weeting. Keep ahead when the track enters the forest to reach the main road.

Turn right along the A1065, walking on its broad verge for about 200 yds

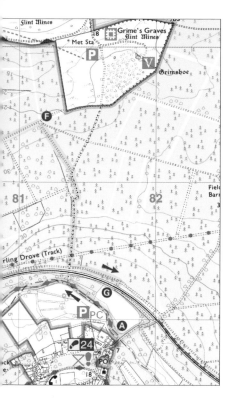

covered by corrugated iron. This is another grassy track which is – after a little distance when it emerges from trees – waymarked for pedestrians and riders. This is a lovely part of the walk in high summer when it seems as though all of Norfolk's butterflies congregate here, including tortoise-shells and common blues. On the other hand, if dusk is falling you are likely to be assaulted by less welcome insects, a species which falls midway between midge and horsefly and seems to have the worst characteristics of both.

Keep following waymarks when another track crosses and as the way begins to descend to the river again. Keep ahead again when another way-marked track leaves to the left. Cross Harling Drove to come to the railway and turn left after crossing the gravel track on to a grassy path that threads its way through gorse bushes and heather before coming to a railway bridge. Pass underneath this and turn left **G** at the informative noticeboard that gives details of the meadow facing you. It is being restored to traditional grazing so that threatened Breckland birds like fieldfare, snipe and siskin can survive. The minute Desmoulins whorl snail (*Vertigo moulinsiana*) struggles on here, practically unknown elsewhere.

Turn right at the road and cross the river to return to the start. ●

(183m) before taking the lane on the left signposted to Grime's Graves.

Some walkers may like to visit the prehistoric flint mines by walking along this road and leaving it at the footpath shown on the map. On their return they will have to navigate southwards from the perimeter fence to reach **F**. This adds at least a mile (1.6km) to the route.

Immediately at the start of this byway **E** there is a fingerpost on the far side pointing to Harling Drove. Take this grassy drive and fork right at a footpath junction to continue on another broad grassy path, which goes over a crossways and passes a rather sinister lookout tower before coming to a junction with a gravel drive. Turn left and walk in an easterly direction for almost exactly 1 mile (1.6km), passing the site of Bromehill Cottage, the build-ing itself having disappeared long ago.

Turn sharply right at a fiveways **F** where there is a forestry signpost bear-ing the number 24 next to a watertank

Remains of Weeting Castle

Warham and Wighton from Wells-Next-The-Sea

Start	Wells harbour
Distance	8½ miles (13.7km)
Approximate time	4 hours
Parking	Harbour car park, Wells-Next-The-Sea
Refreshments	Pubs and cafés at Wells, pub at Warham, pub and seasonal tearoom at Wighton
Ordnance Survey maps	Landranger 132 (North West Norfolk), Explorer 251 (Norfolk Coast Central)

At weekends in summer car parking can be difficult in Wells so it may be easier to begin this route at Wighton, which is a spacious village with room for parking near the church. The walk is a grand mix of country and coast walking, using tracks and byways as well as the coastal path across the salt marshes. Note that the country pubs are often closed in the afternoon.

In 1845 Wells was described as an 'irregularly built seaport town' and the eccentric charm of its streets survives to attract tourists and numbers of senior citizens who choose to retire here, in spite of the biting winter winds.

Head eastwards along the waterfront (The Quay) at Wells, passing the old granary – now apartments – and the chandlery. The granary is a reminder that until recently Wells was a commercial port, with two or three coasters sometimes lining its quay within the memory of the writer. This activity had gone on for nearly 800 years – Ramsey Abbey was given a charter in 1202 allowing grain from its Norfolk farms to be loaded at Wells. The mid-19th century saw Wells at the height of its prosperity when it had a population of 3,500, and 330 cargoes each year were unloaded at the quays.

Keep ahead when the path divides Ⓐ

and pass between boatsheds and workshops before climbing to the top of the embankment. There are wonderful vistas from here to the pines at East Hills (the eastern sand spit that shelters the entrance to Wells harbour) and inland towards Warham and Wighton. If you look down to the edge of the salt-marsh you will see the skeletal remains of one of the coasters that finished its last voyage here. An English Nature noticeboard stands at the point where a path cut across an inlet over a footbridge. East coast weather saw the end of this bridge some time ago and it has never been replaced.

The walking is excellent on springy turf and there is a sheltered seat overlooking Warham Greens, where the path bends inland for a short way. A second noticeboard stands at the end of Garden Drove. Keep on the coast path to the third noticeboard Ⓑ, where a path runs

across the salt marsh towards the sea. Climb the slight rise and turn inland down Cocklestrand Drove, a good sandy track which soon reaches the main road.

Cross the A149 to the lane opposite, which is a quiet byway that climbs directly into Warham and the crossroads by the Three Horseshoes. Go straight across here on a lane that passes Warham's All Saints' Church and first climbs and then drops to a humpbacked bridge. The tower of the other church of the village, dedicated to St Mary Magdalen, can be seen to the right. Also to the right, reached by a bridleway at the top of the hill, is Warham Camp, an Iron Age fort dating from c. 50 BC and covering about 3½ acres (1.4 ha). Twin ditches and earthen ramparts (originally topped by timber palisades) must have made this a conspicuous feature of the windswept landscape.

The lane bends right before dropping into Wighton – there is a good view of the fort before you reach the village. Turn right at the T-junction and pass (or pause at) the Carpenters' Arms before bearing right up the main street to the church. The former school is now an art gallery, and there is a seasonal teashop at the top of the street, open from noon, except Monday and Thursday. Keep ahead on the Wells road, but leave it when it bends right ◉ by keeping straight on along a byway going towards a railway bridge. This spans the narrow-gauge steam railway that runs between Wells and Walsingham. Go over the bridge and past the cemetery.

After this the track is stony and must be hard on the tyres of the many bicycles that use it, but at least the scrunching stones give warning of their approach, and it is pleasant walking

past a patchwork of fields. On a hot day the shade offered by the trees on Gallow Hill is welcome. Take the second track to the right here ◉ to head northwards down to Wells. The high hedges provide excellent blackberries but screen the view. Wells church can be seen ahead as the track passes cattle sheds. Keep ahead when the main track leaves to the right after these.

The path leads past a school playing field, used as a camping field at summer holiday time, and joins the road to the school by another cemetery. Cross the main road and turn left for 20 yds (18m) before turning right up a footpath that takes you up Plummer Hill and into the Buttlands, which is a delightful green faced by early-19th-century houses that were the homes and offices of lawyers, doctors and shipping agents when first built. Cross the grass diagonally to the Globe Inn and then turn right and left to descend Staithe Street, the main thoroughfare, back to the Quay. ●

The Wells–Walsingham train

Castle Rising and Roydon Common

Start	Trinity Hospital, Castle Rising
Distance	10 miles (16.1km)
Approximate time	4½ hours
Parking	On road at start
Refreshments	Pubs at Castle Rising, Congham and Roydon
Ordnance Survey maps	Landranger 132 (North West Norfolk), Explorer 250 (Norfolk Coast West)

Although the length of the walk may appear daunting, this should not deter anyone seeking an excellent day out amidst some of the best and most varied scenery Norfolk has to offer. Note that the going may be muddy along the bank of the Babingley River where the footpath seems to disappear for the last ½ mile (800m) or so. At the halfway point a choice of two pubs is on offer, the first of them a free house.

🖊 Walk northwards along the lane to pass Trinity Hospital on the right and pass a gate that closes the road to vehicular traffic (however, the cats'-eyes remain). The road swings right around a bend picturesquely known as Onion Corner. Keep ahead along the track at the end of the wood to a bridge **A**, but before crossing it, turn right by the white railings on to a delightful path along the riverbank, which may bring you close to all manner of wildlife, such as herons and the enormous black slugs that emerge after rain. The river disappears beneath the main road. Cross the road to a stile opposite and then walk across the meadow to a gate in the far right-hand corner.

Keep ahead on a driveway and, ignoring two paths that go to the right at the end of an evergreen hedge **B**, fork right a few yards further on when the drive swerves to the left. This is a beautiful part of the walk on a woodland track. Eventually it emerges from the woods through a metal gate **C** to enter a meadow. Cross this diagonally to the bank of the river and then turn right to follow it upstream. The going may be boggy at times but the delightful trout stream at your side distracts you from discomfort – you could well be in Scotland for parts of this walk. The path on the riverbank ends at the final field, which proves to be long and may well be planted. Be consoled that this is likely to be the most difficult walking that will be encountered.

Turn right at the lane and right again at the main road. Cross the road to turn left to Roydon **D**. On the edge of Roydon turn left down the lane sign-posted to Congham (St Andrew's Lane). Cross a railway bridge (the railway went from King's Lynn to Fakenham – there is no trace of the trackbed) and keep ahead at a road junction to reach The Anvil, Congham's isolated pub.

If you do not wish to visit this pub take the footpath that strikes across the field on the opposite side of the road from a point just before the pub **E**. After crossing the field, strike across a smaller field to a waymark set at the midpoint of a small wood. Cross a plank bridge and walk through the belt of trees to cross a meadow towards a house. A footpath runs to the left of this to emerge at the road next to the Three Horseshoes at Roydon. The building is made of dark brown carrstone, Norfolk's only natural building stone apart from flint.

Walk past the pub and cross the green by turning left after the garage. Turn right to pass the children's playground. At the T-junction at the end of the road **F** keep ahead on the footpath, which leads to Roydon Common, passing a campsite to the left. After a metal gate there is good walking on a straight, sandy path through birch trees. In late summer you will see colourful toadstools. After $^1\!/_2$ mile (800m) the trackbed of the old railway joins from the right though it is difficult to identify the exact spot. This is a multipurpose right of way used by horsemen and bikers as well as walkers. On this surface bikers come up on you quietly and often quickly so keep a watch for them to the rear.

Cross a stile and turn right on to a

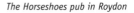

The Horseshoes pub in Roydon

track going past a modern cottage **G** – a concessionary path continues ahead at this point along the old trackbed but is becoming overgrown. The track becomes increasingly sandy as it continues along the edge of the common. Another track leaves to the left through a gatepost into a planting of conifers (Grimston Warren) and 150 yds (137m) further on turn right on to a footpath marked by a Norfolk Wildlife Trust noticeboard **H**. There are wide views across the heather to the right from this path with scarcely a building in sight. Here too one might well be in Scotland.

Go right when the path meets a broad sandy track which takes you to a road. Turn left on to this for 150 yds (137m) and then turn off it to the right over a stile on to a path running down the edge of a field with Scots' pines to the left. After 50 yds (46m) bear left to cross another stile **J** and then turn right to head eastwards on a field-edge path with a hedge to the right. The path climbs and passes a small planting of conifers to the left. It levels out and

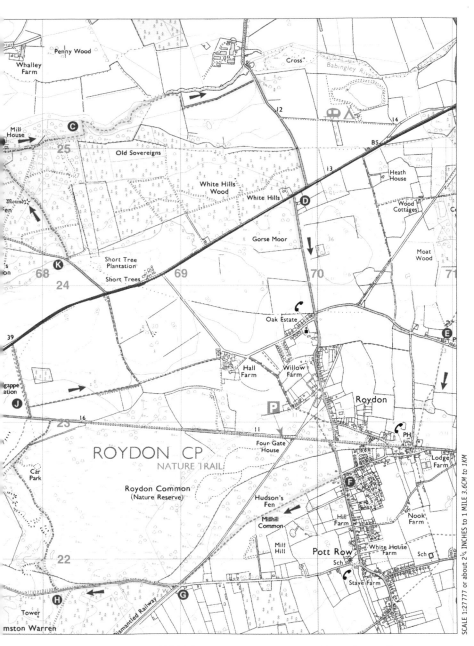

reaches the end of the large field. Turn left here to walk along the eastern edge of the field to reach the main road.

Cross the road to a minor road heading into woodland. Where the road drops suddenly to enter the wood, climb the stile on the right by a gate **K**. Pine-needles underfoot make the walking comfortable as the path winds through trees as it descends. Keep ahead over two crossways and keep descending to reach **B**, the footpath junction by the evergreen hedge. Turn sharp left here to follow a path through the woods and over two plank bridges to the A149 trunk road. Cross directly over this to a field-edge path opposite, which takes you into Castle Rising village. Turn right at the road to return to the starting point. ●

Breydon Water and the Berney Arms

Start	Great Yarmouth rail station
Distance	10 miles (16.1km) – there and back
Approximate time	4 hours
Parking	Car parks in Great Yarmouth
Refreshments	Pub at Berney Arms (mid-March to last Saturday in October), café at Asda superstore near start
Ordnance Survey maps	Landranger 134 (Norwich & The Broads), Explorer OL40 (The Broads)

This is a linear walk, but one that offers a variety of options. It can be walked in either direction though the views west show Breydon Water at its best. On Sundays in summer several trains stop at Berney Arms to take you to Great Yarmouth, Reedham or Norwich. However, if you wish to use the train at other times it is best to start the walk at Yarmouth and continue on the riverbank after Berney Arms for about 2 miles (3.2km) to Reedham. Whatever way, memories of the watery landscape will linger.

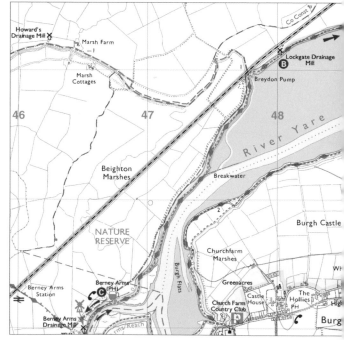

📌 From Great Yarmouth railway station join the sea wall at the Asda supermarket car park and walk along it to pass under the bypass that skirts the western edge of the town. This path is the final section of the 56-mile (90km) -long Weavers Way which links Cromer with Great Yarmouth.

The path passes the first of a series of birdwatchers' hides – the Breydon marshes are a mecca for ornithologists who come to see resident waders as well as a wide range of migrants. The railway is close to the right and the stretch of water called the Lower Drain to the left as the path swings around the eastern end of Breydon, and there is a fine view back to Yarmouth. Ahead the tidal lake seems limitless. After two stiles there is a broad dyke to the right and mudflats on the other side. This is where the two railway lines coming to Yarmouth meet and a footpath leaves to the right 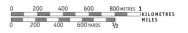 and crosses them to the main road. For some reason it has proved impossible to open an existing track to walkers only 100 yds (91m) long to enable them to return to Yarmouth on the bank of the River Bure.

Walk pass an old ship's lifeboat converted into a bird hide. There is an

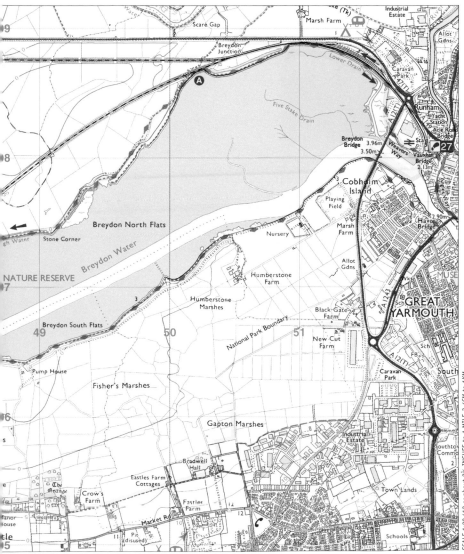

inlet a little way beyond with a tiny beach made of shell sand. After a hide named 'Whimbrel', the bank top – up to now surfaced with concrete blocks with holes to allow grass to grow through – becomes earthen and is covered with thistles. It may be easier to walk along the track at the bottom. In summer, if the tide is favourable, there will be boats passing through Breydon. In winter, without these, the path may seem the loneliest place on earth.

The first notable landmark is the stump of Lockgate Drainage Mill **B**. The ruins of a building, perhaps a marshman's cottage, stand close to it. A little way further on is the modern drainage mill: the Breydon Pump powered by electricity and diesel. A bridleway snakes across the marshes to Halvergate from here and provides a short cut for walkers following the Weavers Way.

A few more minutes' walking takes you to the neck of Breydon Water and a few more to the point where the waters of the Waveney, flowing from Suffolk, merge with those of the Yare. The Berney Arms inn is situated here **C** – it has been a pub for nearly 100 years but before this was a farmhouse. The National Trust owns Berney Arms Mill, the most impressive windpump in the county, standing 70ft (21.3m) tall and dating from 1870. A footpath goes across the marshes from here to the tiny station and then continues to Halvergate. The walk to Reedham along the riverbank will take about an hour.

The marsh landscape near the Berney Arms

Ringstead Downs from Holme next the Sea

Start	Holme next the Sea
Distance	10½ miles (16.9km)
Approximate time	5 hours
Parking	Holme next the Sea car park
Refreshments	Pub at Ringstead, seasonal café at The Firs
Ordnance Survey maps	Landranger 132 (North West Norfolk), Explorer 250 (Norfolk Coast West)

The walk visits two contrasting nature reserves – the first is a small but delightful area of downland that would be acclaimed were it in Kent or Sussex, while the second is a haven for seabirds, waders and migrants. In between there is enjoyable walking on grassy tracks reaching the dizzy height of 164ft (50m).

Leave the car park at its seaward end and turn right along the lane to cross the fairways of the golf course and go through a gateway before coming to the shore. The lagoon here provides excellent bathing if the tide is right. Turn left to walk along the beach heading towards the old lighthouse at Old Hunstanton. Groynes have been made of flints held in wire mesh cages to prevent sand moving southwestwards. After walking for about 1 mile (1.6km) and two groynes before reaching a zigzag fence designed to prevent erosion of the dunes, you will see a noticeboard opposite a groyne, which marks a path **A** through a line of beach huts and then across the golf course. Cross the drive to the clubhouse and enter an enclosed path (known locally as Smugglers' Lane) that crosses a road before reaching another one. Turn right at this T-junction **B** to walk past Caley Hall Motel to the main road.

Cross over to the lane going to the church. The churchyard is worth visiting to see the headstone of poor William Green, 'inumanely murdered' by a gang of smugglers in 1784. The route turns right before the church to climb Chapel Bank. Turn left **C** nearly at the top of the hill at a seat on to a track used by horses. There are fine vistas over the rolling countryside, though the well-maintained hedges sometimes hide the wheat fields and woodland. The straight grassy track makes easy walking. It bends left to skirt Lodge Farm. Turn left when it meets Downs Road but turn sharp right before the Lodge itself **D**.

Another beautiful stretch of track follows through an avenue of old oak and ash trees. The ruins of St Andrew's Chapel are to the right, standing alone in the middle of a field. Bear left at Downs Farm **E**, where there used to be a spring giving intensely cold, iron-rich, water. Fortunately, in view of the adjacent slurry tank, it is now covered. Pass the picturesque cart sheds at the

SCALE 1:31 250 or 2 INCHES to 1 MILE 3.2CM to 1KM

0 200 400 600 800 METRES 1
                              KILOMETRES
                              MILES
0 200 400 600 YARDS ½

farm and keep ahead through a gate into a lovely dry valley, a nature reserve in the care of the Norfolk Wildlife Trust. This is an outstanding part of the walk, a compact example of downland that for beauty is rarely equalled in the chalky uplands of Kent or Sussex. Now that the grass is never cut or grazed, wild flowers are abundant while in the course of about forty years trees have grown up to screen the exposed faces of the chalk pits.

Turn left into Ringstead village. The

Gin Trap Inn is situated a few steps beyond the junction, where the road to Burnham and Docking goes ahead **F**. Take this road and keep ahead again towards Burnham when the road to Docking leaves to the right. After about 1 mile (1.6km) there is a car park on the left, where you can pick up a leaflet about Court-yard Farm, which is devoted to environment-ally friendly agriculture and where the public is given generous access to field paths and tracks.

Continue along the road until a lane goes to the right to Courtyard Farm. Turn left here **G** on a track, which climbs towards the belt of trees known as North Wood. To the right is a field of set-aside land that has been uncultivated since 1993 so it now supports about 30 different species of wild flowers. Turn left to pass through an opening fenced by palings, and then right to climb the footpath on the west side of North Wood. Turn right at the top of the wood on to a path along the edge of a field and then left when this meets a broad track.

Keep ahead when this broad grassy track meets a lane at a triangulation pillar **H** to continue walking north wards, now on a byway that gives wide views over the salt marshes around Thornham. Having dropped to the main road, cross it to a private road opposite,

which ends at a metal gate and stile. Keep ahead on a grassy track – at the end of this the path swings left to cross a ditch. Follow the ditch until about 200 yds (183m) beyond the end of a coppice, where there is a plank bridge taking the right of way to the right-hand side of the ditch. Turn left when the path meets the North Norfolk Coast Long distance Footpath **J**.

Miles of boardwalk have been laid on the dunes to protect them from erosion. The path skirts the seaward shore of Broad Water, a bird sanctuary with hides run by the Norfolk Wildlife Trust from The Firs, where visitors can obtain information about the Holme Dunes Nature Reserve as well as refreshments in the summer months. The path skirts The Firs by going through the beautiful pine trees on its seaward side. It may be tempting to walk on the shore after a path goes left to The Firs, but walkers should be aware that it is not easy to rejoin the coastal path further on due to parts of the foreshore being fenced off to protect nesting-sites. It is best to remain on the boardwalk.

After a car park below on the out-skirts of Holme, the boardwalk ends and the walker can appreciate its benefits. You may prefer to walk on the Firs Approach Road after the car park but will miss the outstanding views along the coast. Either way brings you back. ●

Ringstead Downs

Further Information

The National Trust

Anyone who likes visiting places of natural beauty and/or historic interest has cause to be grateful to the National Trust. Without it, many such places would probably have vanished by now.

It was in response to the pressures on the countryside posed by the relentless march of Victorian industrialisation that the trust was set up in 1895. Its founders, inspired by the common goals of protecting and conserving Britain's national heritage and widening public access to it, were Sir Robert Hunter, Octavia Hill and Canon Rawnsley: respectively a solicitor, a social reformer and a clergyman. The latter was particularly influential. As a canon of Carlisle Cathedral and vicar of Crosthwaite (near Keswick), he was concerned about threats to the Lake District and had already been active in protecting footpaths and promoting public access to open countryside. After the flooding of Thirlmere in 1879 to create a large reservoir, he became increasingly convinced that the only effective way to guarantee protection was outright ownership of land.

The purpose of the National Trust is to preserve areas of natural beauty and sites of historic interest by acquisition, holding them in trust for the nation and making them available for public access and enjoyment. Some of its properties have been acquired through purchase, but many of the Trust's properties have been donated. Nowadays it is not only one of the biggest landowners in the country, but also one of the most active conservation charities, protecting 581,113 acres (253,176 ha) of land, including 555 miles (892km) of coastline, and over 300 historic properties in England, Wales and Northern Ireland. (There is a separate National Trust for Scotland, which was set up in 1931.)

Furthermore, once a piece of land has come under National Trust ownership, it is difficult for its status to be altered. As a result of parliamentary legislation in 1907, the Trust was given the right to declare its property inalienable, so ensuring that in any subsequent dispute it can appeal directly to parliament.

As it works towards its dual aims of conserving areas of attractive countryside and encouraging greater public access (not easy to reconcile in this age of mass tourism), the Trust provides an excellent service for walkers by creating new concessionary paths and waymarked trails, maintaining stiles and foot bridges and combating the ever-increasing problem of footpath erosion.

For details of membership, contact the National Trust at the address on page 95.

The Ramblers' Association

No organisation works more actively to protect and extend the rights and interests of walkers in the countryside than the Ramblers' Association. Its aims are clear: to foster a greater knowledge, love and care of the countryside; to assist in the protection and enhancement of public rights of way and areas of natural beauty; to work for greater public access to the countryside; and to encourage more people to take up rambling as a healthy, recreational leisure activity.

It was founded in 1935 when, following the setting up of a National Council of Ramblers' Federations in 1931, a number of federations earlier formed in London, Manchester, the Midlands and elsewhere came together to create a more effective pressure group, to deal with such problems as the disappearance and obstruction of footpaths, the prevention of access to open mountain and moorland and increasing hostility from landowners. This was the era of the mass trespasses, when there were sometimes violent

The River Babingley, Castle Rising

confrontations between ramblers and gamekeepers, especially on the moorlands of the Peak District.

Since then the Ramblers' Association has played an influential role in preserving and developing the national footpath network, supporting the creation of national parks and encouraging the designation and waymarking of long-distance routes.

Our freedom to walk in the countryside is precarious and requires constant vigilance. As well as the perennial problems of footpaths being illegally obstructed, disappearing through lack of use or extinguished by housing or road construction, new dangers can spring up at any time.

It is to meet such problems and dangers that the Ramblers' Association exists and represents the interests of all walkers. The address to write to for information on the Ramblers' Association and how to become a member is given on page 95.

Walkers and the Law

The average walker in a national park or other popular walking area, armed with the appropriate Ordnance Survey map, reinforced perhaps by a guidebook giving detailed walking instructions, is unlikely to run into legal difficulties, but it is useful to know something about the law relating to public rights of way. The right to walk over certain parts of the countryside has developed over a long period, and how such rights came into being is a complex subject, too lengthy to be discussed here. The following comments are intended simply as a helpful guide, backed up by the Countryside Access Charter, a concise summary of walkers' rights and obligations drawn up by the Countryside Agency (see page 94).

Basically there are two main kinds of public rights of way: footpaths (for walkers only) and bridleways (for walkers, riders on horseback and pedal cyclists). Footpaths and bridleways are shown by broken green lines on Ordnance Survey Explorer maps and broken red lines on Landranger maps. There is also a third category, called byways: chiefly broad tracks (green lanes) or farm roads, which walkers, riders and cyclists have to share, usually only occasionally, with motor vehicles. Many of these public paths have been in existence for hundreds of years and some even originated as prehistoric trackways and have been in constant use for well over 2,000 years. Ways known as

Countryside Access Charter

Your rights of way are:

- public footpaths – on foot only. Sometimes waymarked in yellow
- bridleways – on foot, horseback and pedal cycle. Sometimes waymarked in blue
- byways (usually old roads), most 'roads used as public paths' and, of course, public roads – all traffic has the right of way

Use maps, signs and waymarks to check rights of way. Ordnance Survey Explorer and Landranger maps show most public rights of way

On rights of way you can:

- take a pram, pushchair or wheelchair if practicable
- take a dog (on a lead or under close control)
- take a short route round an illegal obstruction or remove it sufficiently to get past

You have a right to go for recreation to:

- public parks and open spaces – on foot
- most commons near older towns and cities – on foot and sometimes on horseback
- private land where the owner has a formal agreement with the local authority

In addition you can use the following by local or established custom or consent, but ask for advice if you are unsure:

- many areas of open country, such as moorland, fell and coastal areas, especially those in the care of the National Trust, and some commons
- some woods and forests, especially those owned by the Forestry Commission
- country parks and picnic sites
- most beaches
- canal towpaths
- some private paths and tracks Consent sometimes extends to horse-riding and cycling

For your information:

- county councils and London boroughs maintain and record rights of way, and register commons
- obstructions, dangerous animals, harassment and misleading signs on rights of way are illegal and you should report them to the county council
- paths across fields can be ploughed, but must normally be reinstated within two weeks
- landowners can require you to leave land to which you have no right of access
- motor vehicles are normally permitted only on roads, byways and some 'roads used as public paths'

RUPPs (roads used as public paths) still appear on some maps. The legal definition of such byways is ambiguous and they are gradually being reclassified as footpaths, bridleways or byways.

The term 'right of way' means exactly what it says. It gives right of passage over what, in the vast majority of cases, is private land, and you are required to keep to the line of the path and not stray on to the land on either side. If you inadvertently wander off the right of way – either because of faulty map-reading or because the route is not clearly indicated on the ground – you are technically trespassing and the wisest course is to ask the nearest available person (farmer or fellow walker) to direct you back to the correct route.

There are stories about unpleasant confrontations between walkers and farmers at times, but in general most farmers are co-operative when responding to a genuine and polite request for assistance in route-finding.

Obstructions can sometimes be a problem and probably the most common of these is where a path across a field has been ploughed up. It is legal for a farmer to plough up a path provided that he restores it within two weeks, barring exceptionally bad weather. This does not always happen and here the walker is presented with a dilemma: to follow the line of the path, even if this inevitably means treading on crops, or to walk around the edge of the field. The latter course of action often seems the best but this means that you would be trespassing and not keeping to the exact line of the path. In the case of other obstructions which may block a path (illegal fences and locked gates etc), common sense has to be used in order to negotiate them by the easiest method – detour or removal. You should only ever remove as much as is necessary to get through, and if you can easily go round the obstruction without causing any damage, then you should do so. If you have any problems negotiating rights of way, you should report the matter to the rights of way department of the relevant council, which will take action with the landowner concerned.

Apart from rights of way enshrined by law, there are a number of other paths available to walkers. Permissive or concessionary paths have been created where a landowner has given permission for the public to use a particular route across his land. The main problem with these is that, as they have been granted as a concession, there is no legal right to use them and therefore they can be extinguished at any time. In practice, many of these concessionary routes have

been established on land owned either by large public bodies such as the Forestry Commission, or by a private one, such as the National Trust, and as these mainly encourage walkers to use their paths, they are unlikely to be closed unless a change of ownership occurs.

Walkers also have free access to country parks (except where requested to keep away from certain areas for ecological reasons, e.g wildlife protection, woodland regeneration, etc), canal towpaths and most beaches. By custom, though not by right, you are generally free to walk across the open and uncultivated higher land of mountain, moorland and fell, but this varies from area to area and from one season to another – grouse moors, for example, will be out of bounds during the breeding and shooting seasons and some open areas are used as Ministry of Defence firing ranges, for which reason access will be restricted. In some areas the situation has been clarified as a result of 'access agreements' between the landowners and either the county council or the national park authority, which clearly define when and where you can walk over such open country.

Saxlingham Old Hall

Walking Safety

Although the reasonably gentle countryside that is the subject of this book offers no real dangers to walkers at any time of the year, it is still advisable to take sensible precautions and follow certain well-tried guidelines.

Always take with you both warm and waterproof clothing and sufficient food and drink. Wear suitable footwear such as strong walking boots or shoes that give a good grip over stony ground, on slippery slopes and in muddy conditions. Try to obtain a local weather forecast and bear it in mind before you start. Do not be afraid to abandon your proposed route and return to your starting point in the event of a sudden and unexpected deterioration in the weather.

All the walks described in this book will be safe to do, given due care and respect, even during the winter. Indeed, a crisp, fine winter day often provides perfect walking conditions, with firm ground underfoot and a clarity unique to this time of the year. The most difficult hazard likely to be encountered is mud, especially when walking along woodland and field paths, farm tracks and bridleways – the latter in particular can often get churned up by cyclists and horses. In summer, an additional difficulty may be narrow and overgrown paths, particularly along the edges of cultivated fields. Neither should constitute a major problem provided that the appropriate footwear is worn.

Useful Organisations

Council for the Protection of Rural England
128 Southwark Street, London SE1 0SW.
Tel. 020 7981 2800

Countryside Agency
John Dower House, Crescent Place, Cheltenham, Gloucestershire GL50 3RA.
Tel. 01242 521381

Forestry Commission
Information Branch, 231 Corstorphine Rd, Edinburgh EH12 7AT.
Tel. 0131 334 0303
Thetford Forest District Office:
Santon Downham, Brandon, Suffolk IP27 OTJ.
Tel. 01842 810271

Long Distance Walkers' Association
Bank House, High Street, Wrotham, Sevenoaks, Kent TN15 7AE .
Tel. 01732 883705

Sunset on the River Ant at How Hill

Council for National Parks
246 Lavender Hill, London SW11 1LJ.
Tel. 020 7924 4077

The Broads Authority
18 Colegate, Norwich NR3 1BQ.
Tel. 01603 610734
*Broads Authority information centres
(open Easter to October):*
Beccles: 01502 713196
Great Yarmouth (July–September):
01493 846345
Hoveton/Wroxham: 01603 782281
How Hill, Ludham: 01692 678763
Ranworth: 01603 270453

National Trust
Membership and general enquiries:
PO Box 39, Bromley, Kent BR1 3XL.
Tel. 0870 458 4000
East Anglia Regional Office:
Blickling, Norwich NR11 6NF.
Tel. 0870 609 5388

Norfolk County Council
County Hall, Martineau Lane,
Norwich NR1 2DH.
Bridleways and footpaths: 01603 223284
Regional Planning Dept: 01603 222143

Ordnance Survey
Romsey Road, Maybush,
Southampton SO16 4GU.
Tel. 08456 05 05 05 (Lo-call)

Ramblers' Association
2nd Floor, Camelford House,
87–90 Albert Embankment,
London SE1 7TW.
Tel. 020 7339 8500

Tourist information:
East of England Tourist Board,
Toppesfield Hall, Hadleigh,
Suffolk IP7 5DN.
Tel. 01473 822922
*Local tourist information offices (*not
open all year):*
Cromer: 01263 512497
Diss: 01379 650523
*Fakenham: 01328 851981
Great Yarmouth: 01493 846345

Ipswich: 01473 258070
King's Lynn: 01553 763044
Lowestoft: 01502 523000
Norwich: 01603 727927
*Sheringham: 01263 824329
Wells-Next-The-Sea: 01328 710885

Youth Hostels Association
Trevelyan House, Dimple Road, Matlock,
Derbyshire DE4 3YH.
Tel. 01629 592600

Weather forecasts:
Weathercall (Met office forecast by phone)
Tel. 09014 722058

 **Ordnance Survey
Maps of Norfolk**
The area of Norfolk is covered by Ordnance
Survey 1:50 000 (1¼ inches to 1 mile or 2cm
to 1km) scale Landranger map sheets 132,
133, 134, 143, 144 and 156. These all-
purpose maps are packed with information
to help you explore the area and show view-
points, picnic sites, places of interest and
caravan and camping sites.
   To examine the Norfolk area in more detail
and especially if you are planning walks,
Ordnance Survey Explorer maps at 1:25 000
(2½ inches to 1 mile or 4cm to 1km) scale
are ideal:

   228 March & Ely
   229 Thetford Forest in The Brecks
   230 Diss & Harleston
   236 King's Lynn, Downham Market
      & Swaffham
   237 Norwich
   238 East Dereham & Aylsham
   250 Norfolk Coast West
   251 Norfolk Coast Central
   252 Norfolk Coast East

The Explorer map OL40 (The Broads) at
1:25 000 scale is also helpful.
   To get to the Norfolk area use the Ordnance
Survey OS Travel Map-Route Great Britain at
1:625 000 (1 inch to 10 miles or 4cm to
25km) scale or the OS Travel Map-Road 5
(East Midlands and East Anglia including
London) at 1:250 000 (1 inch to 4 miles or
1cm to 2.5km) scale.
   Ordnance Survey maps and guides are
available from most booksellers, stationers
and newsagents.

www.totalwalking.co.uk

www.totalwalking.co.uk
is the official website of the Jarrold
Pathfinder and Short Walks guides. This
interactive website features a wealth of
information for walkers – from the latest
news on route diversions and advice from
professional walkers to product news, free
sample walks and promotional offers.